W9-ADB-071

ARTHURIAN STUDIES XXVII

SIR GAWAIN AND THE GREEN KNIGHT
Sources and Analogues

ARTHURIAN STUDIES

ISSN 0261-9814

Previously published volumes in the series
are listed at the back of this book

SIR GAWAIN
AND THE
GREEN KNIGHT

Sources and Analogues

COMPILED BY

Elisabeth Brewer

D. S. BREWER

First published 1973 as *From Cuchulainn to Gawain*
by D. S. Brewer, Cambridge
Second edition 1992 as
Sir Gawain and the Green Knight: Sources and Analogues

D. S. Brewer is an imprint of Boydell & Brewer Ltd
PO Box 9, Woodbridge, Suffolk IP12 3DF, UK
and of Boydell & Brewer Inc.
PO Box 41026, Rochester, NY 14604, USA

ISBN 0 85991 358 9 hardback
ISBN 0 85991 359 7 paperback

British Library Cataloguing-in-Publication Data
Sir Gawain and the Green Knight: Sources
and Analogues. – 2 Rev.ed. – (Arthurian
Studies Series, ISSN 0261-9814; Vol. 27)
I. Brewer, Elisabeth II. Series
821.1
ISBN 0-85991-358-9
ISBN 0-85991-359-7 pbk

Library of Congress Cataloging-in-Publication Data applied for

The paper used in this publication meets the minimum requirements
of American National Standard for Information Sciences –
Permanence of Paper for Printed Library Materials, ANSI Z39.48–1984

Printed in Great Britain by
St Edmundsbury Press Ltd, Bury St Edmunds, Suffolk

Contents

Introduction

I schal telle hit as-tit, as I in toun herde,
with tonge

says the *Gawain*-poet as he begins his tale, and whether one takes
him literally or not, there is no doubt that he is handing on a story
of which a number of elements were already well-known, and
had provided powerful ingredients, with variations, im many a
tale across Europe throughout the Middle Ages.

The story of Gawain's courage and integrity in accepting the
challenge of the green stranger to cut off his head, in return for a
similar blow in a year's time, with the lady's temptations which
turn out to be so closely connected with the ultimate obligation, is
told with remarkable realism and has the power of myth. *Sir
Gawain and the Green Knight* can be enjoyed simply for itself, even
in translation, but it gains in interest when it is seen in the context
of the other poems and episodes with which it has features in
common. It is the aim of this collection to provide something of
the poem's context in earlier and later medieval French and
English literature.

The earliest recorded version of the beheading game occurs in
the Middle Irish prose narrative, *Bricriu's Feast*, followed here by
those other examples of the topos (with the exception of the
German *Lanzelet* and *Diu Crône* which the *Gawain*-poet is unlikely
to have known) that are generally considered to be either possible
sources or close analogues of *Sir Gawain and the Green Knight*. Of
these, the story of Carados from the Continuations of Chretien's
Perceval, given here in different versions, most closely cor-
responds with the beheading episodes in the English poem. The
same common theme (better called a topos) appears, in connection with both Lancelot and Gawain in *Perlesvaus*, while in *The
Girl with the Mule* and *Hunbaut* Gawain is required to decapitate
an adversary. The tradition continues in the Prose Redaction with
a much later version of the story of Carados. As all these

1

examples are in a variety of Old French dialects, they have been translated in the following pages.

There are a number of other features of *Sir Gawain and the Green Knight* beside the beheading game for which analogues can be found in medieval literature, primarily of course the temptation theme, of which several examples have been given. More analogues for some other important passages in the poem have been added in this edition.

Many medieval authors chose to describe feasts in their narratives, and the feast in the alliterative *Morte Arthure* is a particularly sumptuous example, in which a menu more elaborate but of the same kind as in *Sir Gawain and the Green Knight* is supplied for the listeners' or readers' delectation.

The passing of the year at the beginning of Fitt II suggests that the poet may have been familiar with the passage describing the seasons in the *Secretum Secretorum*, of which two versions have been given.

The arming of Gawain before his departure from Arthur's court belongs in the tradition of the ritual arming of the warrior represented here by such passages as those from *Erec and Enide* and *Winner and Waster*, while the vivid description of the hunting of the deer has its counterpart in the *Awntyrs of Arthur*. The very detailed account of the breaking of the deer after the first day's hunt has some similarities with a passage in *The Book of St Albans*.

The *Gawain*-poet could also have found in both earlier and contemporary stories many other traditional motifs to work into his own poem, such as the perilous and testing journey, the welcome at the castle, Morgan le Fay's trouble-making and Gawain's misogynistic outburst. Their recurrence in his poem throws interesting light on the complex of feelings on which the story rests, and on medieval methods of story-telling.

The number of correspondences between the Grail narratives of *Perceval* and *Perlesvaus* and *Sir Gawain and the Green Knight*, however, are so numerous as to suggest that the *Gawain*-poet must at least have heard these tales and found expressed in them an ideal of knighthood close to his own. For Chrétien in his *Perceval* the development of the spiritual alongside the martial aspect of the knight was of the utmost importance, as Nigel Bryant has pointed out.[1] Perceval as a supremely fine knight in

[1] *Perceval: The Story of the Grail: Chrétien de Troyes*, translated by Nigel Bryant, Cambridge 1982.

moral and spiritual as well as military terms embodies Chrétien's ideal, but Gawain as a participant in the Grail-quest is also presented by Chrétien as aspiring to it.

In *Perceval*, Chrétien represents Gawain as courteous, brave and chaste, a knight who will keep his word, cost what it may, once it has been given. His Gawain takes a vow to search for the lance whose head sheds drops of blood, and his journey takes him through wild country to a great castle where he sees not only the lance, but the Holy Grail itself, borne aloft by a beautiful girl. He is then tested by the lord who asks him to piece together the broken sword. Gawain is unable to complete the task satisfactorily and so cannot receive the full revelation because, listening with intense concentration to what the lord has to say to him, he inadvertently falls asleep and wakes to find himself alone in the wild countryside with only his horse and his armour. He is aghast and ashamed at the realisation of his failure to 'learn the truth about the mysteries'; but his distress is much increased by his recollection that he has a promise to keep, since he has given his word that he will return to Escavalon with the bleeding lance or else engage in combat with Guigambresil.

This association of Gawain with the Holy Grail, his deep sense of shame at his failure, and his commitment to his promise suggest a rather differently conceived character from the more frivolous Gawain of the later stories such as *The Knight of the Sword* (*Le Chevalier à L'Epée*). Later, in *Sir Gawain and the Green Knight*, the English poet confronts the spiritually-minded Gawain of *Perceval*, as it were, with the sexual adventures which were more frequently associated with him in the later romances.

Perceval and the poem's First Continuation, in addition to representing Gawain as an ideal knight, contain between them a very large amount of material which the *Gawain*-poet could have used, from the major episode of the beheading scene in the Carados story, to the minute details of castle customs. Some of these motifs may be seen as the common stuff of romance, but the fact that so many occur in this text clustered around the Gawain and Carados stories seems to suggest that the *Gawain*-poet knew these stories, though he borrowed nothing from their plots. Such later works as *Gawain and the Carl of Carlisle* are so garbled that they give the impression that their authors must have heard *Sir Gawain and the Green Knight* and tried to re-tell it, while remembering it only imperfectly. To read *Sir Gawain and the Green*

Knight itself, as opposed to its presumed derivatives, is to be impressed by its remarkable coherence and power. The poet has brilliantly re-shaped, re-structured, re-combined and generally put together far more dramatically, with more intense and concentrated meaningfulness, the things he says that he heard 'in toun', or, more likely, read in the French romances.

The most significant correspondence between *Perceval* and the Middle English poem is the Carados story. Many other minor features of *Perceval* also have their counterpart in *Sir Gawain and the Green Knight*, for example, Gawain's departure from the court. These resemblances are mostly on a small scale, only to be fully grasped in a continuous reading of *Perceval*, but in such a reading their accumulated force is irresistible as an argument for the *Gawain*-poet's knowledge of the poem. As they do not lend themselves to itemised translation a brief account of them is given here.

As Perceval sets out on his quest to discover who is served from the Grail and to find the bleeding lance (51), Gawain is accused of treachery by Guigambresil and leaves the court with the intention of vindicating himself. His going is marked by the same sort of sorrow as is expressed when his counterpart leaves Camelot to search for the Green Chapel:

> Before he had even left the court there was bitter grieving for him, as many beat their breasts and tore their hair and scratched their faces in despair; there was no lady, however cool-headed, who did not grieve for him desperately. Many men and women lamented bitterly as Sir Gawain departed.

Later he engages in love-talk. He comes to a castle where he is mortally hated by everyone, but not recognised, and here he is enthusiastically welcomed by a lovely girl. Alone together, they both talk of love – 'if they had talked of anything else, what a waste of breath it would have been' – but their love-making has gone no further than kissing before they are interrupted by a servant. That Gawain is a model of chastity is apparent from the innocence of this encounter, emphasised when it is later suggested that he has been disgracefully treated by the mob who attack at the instigation of this servant.

As in *Sir Gawain and the Green Knight*, the quest of Chrétien's Gawain results from a binding oath, and is governed by a strict time-limit. Gawain goes on his way again, after swearing an oath that he will do his utmost to find the bleeding lance, returning to imprisonment in a year's time if he is unable to do so. In his next encounter, at the castle with the two queens and the Marvellous Bed, there appear several motifs later to be found in *Sir Gawain and the Green Knight*. Like the Green Knight's castle of Haut Desert, the castle in *Perceval* though delightful in many respects is a place of danger which stems chiefly from the bed itself. It is claimed that no knight can rest on it and remain alive; however, Gawain manages to survive the various attacks with which he is assailed when he attempts to sleep on it. After the ordeal, he is welcomed, disarmed and dressed in magnificent clothes, then goes with his host to view the surrounding countryside from the top of a tower. The forests are full of wild beasts, which he longs to hunt, but his host tells him that he cannot leave the castle, so that such sport is out of the question. Angered, he returns to the hall, where he is met by two queens: one is a grandmother while the other is young, just as Morgan le Fay and Lady Bertilak differ in age (though the elder lady, presumably because she is 'good', does not have the repellent appearance attributed to Morgan). One of these queens turns out to be Gawain's own mother, while the other is the mother of King Arthur.

In *Perceval*, as in *Sir Gawain and the Green Knight*, Gawain goes to confession. After the adventure of the Marvellous Bed, the day comes for him to do battle, so before the dangerous encounter he confesses his sins to a bishop called Solomon, is given full absolution, and told to have faith in God as his protector, after which he prepares for the fight. An account of his arming follows: it is not as detailed as that in *Sir Gawain and the Green Knight*, but provides a sketch which a later writer could develop. Gawain puts on a padded doublet under his armour and is provided with all the necessary weapons for attack and defence, while his horse is brought out in splendid condition. Again, he goes on his way, passing through a deep wood and coming to a river with rocky banks; not knowing how to get across, he sees to his relief a castle – the Grail castle, as it turns out to be. Here he finds a welcome similar to that extended to him at Bertilak's castle, and often elsewhere in these romances. His horse is taken away to be cared for appropriately, and then his armour is removed and he is offered a fine gown and led to the hall, where dinner is soon served in style.

The arrival at the castle and the subsequent welcome by the
inhabitants is a topos which seems to be frequently associated
with Gawain in these narratives. His reputation for courtesy is
established early in *Perceval*, when he is commended by King
Arthur for this particular quality, and, since he is already famous
and highly honoured for his knightly virtues, it is perhaps not
surprising that he should be received with warmth and respect on
arrival at a castle. While Perceval similarly also often receives a
hearty welcome when he seeks lodging at nightfall, particularly in
the Continuations where he is a fully-fledged knight, it is
frequently at a hermitage or some strange deserted place where
the customary rituals cannot be carried out, as distinct from the
more conventional castles to which Gawain comes. The elaborate
ceremony, rejoicing and feasting with which Gawain is usually
received suggest the familiar world of chivalry to which he
belongs, with its well established traditions and customs, rather
than the more spiritually-oriented background appropriate to
Perceval, who is ultimately to achieve the Grail-quest.

As in Chrétien's *Perceval*, so too in *Perlesvaus* by an unknown
author of the first half of the thirteenth century, there are many
motifs which suggest a tradition with which the *Gawain*-poet
must have been familiar, and he may very well have known the
poem. The beheading game appears again, but this time in
connection with Lancelot. Again we see a noble and spiritually-
minded Gawain engaged in a high quest, praying to God to guide
him as he rides towards the land of the Fisher King through a
great forest. Through the branches, once again, he eventually
sees a castle where he finds a welcome. He is immediately
recognised, then his armour is removed and he is given water for
washing, and provided with a splendid robe. He dines with a
lady of surpassing and almost irresistible beauty, 'but because of
the high pilgrimage he had undertaken he had so bound and
restrained his heart that he would not permit any thoughts to
turn to baseness'.

The situation is very different from that in *Sir Gawain and the
Green Knight* when Gawain is tempted by the lady, since in
Perlesvaus the theme of potential marital infidelity is explicitly
introduced. The domestic dwarf (who has seemed to be
benevolent, contrary to Gawain's expectations) turns out to be
vilely treacherous and falsely informs the lady's husband that she
has slept with her guest. Enraged with jealousy, he savagely

attacks his wife – not Gawain – and kills her before Gawain can stop him.

In the course of his subsequent adventures the question of Gawain's identity is raised as in the first temptation by the Lady, as well as in the comment of the Green Knight at the Green Chapel, 'Thow art not Gawayn'. In *Perlesvaus* Gawain comes to a clearing where a magnificent tent has been put up, furnished with everything necessary for the comfort of the occupant. Again he is welcomed and first served by a dwarf, then by two boys and two maidens, who look to him to bring to an end the evil custom of the tent. To do this he is to choose one of the maidens, and both attend him as he goes and lies down on the rich couch. But, since his only desire is for rest after a hard day, he merely thanks them before apparently falling asleep immediately. The maidens are disgusted, and loudly call in question his identity:

> if this were Gawain, the nephew of King Arthur, he would speak
> to us differently, and we should find in him more entertainment
> than in this man: this man is an impostor.[2]

He hears all their remarks refusing to accept that he really is Gawain; and unable to sleep well, he gets up early, arms himself and rides off. After this adventure he reaches the Fisher King's castle and as in *Perceval*, has a vision of the Grail, but is unable to speak when he should do so, thus preventing the restoration of joy to the castle. He has in consequence to ride through the Perilous Forest, 'the road taken by all those who have failed' (81). Like the later Gawain, he is deeply distressed and mortified by his failure, though in this case his failure is genuine, if understandable.

As he is presented in *Sir Gawain and the Green Knight*, Gawain thus has many similarities with his earlier counterparts in both *Perceval* and *Perlesvaus*. A knight with high spiritual ideals, he yet seems both open to sexual temptation and strong enough to resist it; he also has a well-established reputation for courtesy and courage to preserve. In the Middle English poem, however, he is brought further into the foreground and allowed to become an individual whose hopes, anxieties and fears are made subtly apparent. The Pentangle, uniquely here devised for him as his

[2] From *The High Book of the Grail: A translation of the 13th-century romance of Perlesvaus* by Nigel Bryant, Cambridge 1978, p. 64.

emblem, defines his aspirations. In his inability to live up to them completely he is truly human. We see his courtesy in action, and challenged; we see his disgust at what appears to him as failure finding unbridled expression, and his shame put in perspective by the loving and admiring reception he receives on his return to Camelot.

The extracts and poems in this collection suggest not only something of what the *Gawain*-poet had to draw on, but also how stories were told in the Middle Ages, while at the same time they indicate what the expectations of the original audience might have been. It is obvious from the large number of different versions, in particular of the beheading game, in circulation in the thirteenth and fourteenth centuries that the most important episodes in *Sir Gawain and the Green Knight* were probably widely known and part of the stock-in-trade of storytellers, and may well have appeared in different ways in other stories that have not survived. But in those that have, we can see a good motif being used again and again, attached to different characters, and given new accretions of detail and new significances; a process which emphasises the memorability as well as the popularity of these features.

The material included here also makes very clear how much better the *Gawain*-poet is than the other writers who handle these themes. The beheading-game is the perfect episode for a tale of chivalry, and it is easy to see why it should have appeared in so many different forms. Its usefulness is illustrated by the fact that it occurs in the stories of several different knights. Cuchulainn, Carados, Lancelot as well as Gawain are all confronted in turn by a fearsome challenger. The encounter provides an exciting scene which very efficiently tests both the individual hero and often his society too in no uncertain way, with a breath-taking moment of suspense when the challenger reaches for his head and either holds it up, as in *Sir Gawain and the Green Knight*, or puts it back, as in the story of Carados, or even fails to reach it in time as in *Hunbaut*. The *Gawain*-poet's brilliant addition of significant detail, however, makes his version very much more powerful than the others. The sudden and startling revelation that the challenger is 'overal enker-grene' after the elaborate build-up, the well-realised details of the reactions of the spectators, the delicate and formal courtesy of Gawain in requesting to be allowed to undertake the challenge, the vividly suggested horror of the scene when the head rolls away and 'fele hit foyned wyth her fete, there hit forth roled', and the frightful fact that it is a still-severed head that speaks, make this beheading scene far more impressive than any of the others. But appreciation of its brilliance is increased by knowledge of the other versions, and of the whole tradition of medieval story-telling (just as the character of Gawain gains in subtlety and interest from being seen in the light of his other appearances in Arthurian romance): will the Green Knight be able to pick his head up again – or not?

The temptation analogues seem less close to *Sir Gawain and the Green Knight* than the beheading ones, and one does not feel that they are in any way closely connected with each other. All of them, however, are alike in that there is an element of humour in them. Lancelot has trouble with an over-persistent maiden supplied by Morgan le Fay, and is obliged to rebuff her vigorously by physical means when all else fails. Yder, in a delightfully amusing episode, defends himself from the determined queen (against whose advances he has been warned) to the prudently suppressed mirth of the courtly onlookers. In *Le Chevalier à l'Epée*, Gawain is threatened by the magic sword above his bed, which descends rapidly, unexpectedly and dangerously when he is unable to resist going too far with his imperious host's beautiful naked daughter; though what it makes him anxious about is his reputation – as an aggressive and successful lover, for this Gawain is much less spiritually minded.

As with the beheading game, the *Gawain*-poet is much more skilful than his predecessors in the handling of this theme. The comedy as well as the seriousness of Gawain's situation and the subtlety of the fraught verbal exchanges between the knight and the Lady go far beyond anything in the other temptation-scenes. His reputation as an exponent of 'luf-talkyng' also plays its part in building up suspense and expectation when the Lady visits him in the bedroom.

To read the analogues of *Sir Gawain and the Green Knight* is not only to be aware of the poet's skill in handling traditional episodes, but also to realise how much he added in the way of narrative and descriptive material. The beginning and end of the poem, with its historical perspective, the passing of the year, the arming of the knight – although a well-known topos, not one of which other writers who are concerned with the beheading game make use – the description of the Pentangle, the exchange of winnings and the hunts are examples of the additions – most of them traditional in some sense, but new to the context of the beheading game and the temptation theme.

The bringing together of many different elements and blending them into a new story, and above all, the fusing of the beheading-temptation-exchange-of-winnings themes, illustrate the *Gawain*-poet's genius in devising a very well articulated plot in which symmetry and patterning communicate subtle meanings. Comparison with the poems given here in their entirety, *The Girl with the Mule* (*La Demoiselle à la Mule*) and *The Knight of the Sword* (*Le Chevalier à l'Epée*), makes clear that whatever else he borrowed, he did not borrow his structure from them. They have charm and in each the narrative is well sustained, but in comparison with *Sir Gawain and the Green Knight* they seem to ramble. When we consider the various poetic excellencies of the *Gawain*-poet, as seen by comparison with analogues or possible sources, the theory that he could not have had the genius to combine for himself the beheading game with the theme of temptation, and that he must have used a now-lost French romance which made the connection for him is unconvincing and unnecessary. There seems no reason whatever, when we recognise the genius of the *Gawain*-poet, to deny this aspect of his achievement when there is absolutely no evidence to the contrary.

There is also, as one might expect, no model among the analogues and possible sources for the elaborate stanza-form which the *Gawain*-poet used. Most of them were written in octosyllabic couplets, obviously a convenient free-flowing form for an extended narrative, but a very limiting form, too, which makes subtle effects and all but the simplest description very difficult. It also restricts the possibilities as far as tone and atmosphere are concerned. The later English Gawain-stories are stanzaic, but simply tell the story in a jog-trot, perfunctory way, missing many important elements.

The careful articulation of the plot of *Sir Gawain and the Green Knight* allows the poet to attach more significance to the various incidents of which it is made up. They have an inevitability, a credibility, they create an illusion of reality because of the way in which event is supported by human reaction, observed with psychological truth. It is this psychological perception, above all else, which makes the poem the masterpiece it is; and this perception, though of course apparent to some extent in some of the other extracts and poems, is never more than rudimentary in them. The patterns of repetition and variation, so beautifully constructed in *Sir Gawain and the Green Knight*, the framing perspective at beginning and end and the whole organisation of the poem deepen and emphasise the total meaning of what it is to be Gawain, and what it is to be human as well. The poet's command of tone which ranges from fabliau-type humour to philosophical reflection and takes in such nuances of feeling as irritation, embarrassment and shame, has no precedent in any of the earlier works.

Sir Gawain and the Green Knight, though it has survived in only one manuscript, was apparently more widely known than this would suggest, especially in the North of England. *The Green Knight* and *Sir Gawain and the Carl of Carlisle* make clear that there were memories of the poem, on the strength of which storytellers tried to tell it again. They remembered the most striking incidents such as the beheading game, the temptation, the exchange of winnings, perhaps, but could not reconstruct the logic of the story, or recapture its subtleties or its meaning. These poems make, at the same time, sad and amusing reading.

Where texts in Middle English are accessible without excessive annotation, they have been given in the original; where they present substantial problems, they have been translated. There are two exceptions: *Sir Tristrem* is given in the original, with glosses, because of the technical terms used, and *The Grene Knight* is given in parallel text, because it is the most direct (though very corrupt) analogue. The texts that I have translated here have, of course, lost by being rendered in rather literal prose. It is impossible to find really satisfactory modern equivalents for much of the terminology of thirteenth-century chivalry, and the verbal exchanges of knights and ladies. Feelings and attitudes change as well as fashions: to give only one example, the queen can say to the knight who is proposing to behead Carados, 'When you have given me his *death* you will be well rewarded.' To substitute 'life' for 'death' would be to obliterate an example of a significant and interesting cultural change.

Further Reading

The problem of the exact relationship of *Sir Gawain and the Green Knight* with its analogues and possible sources is not discussed here. But see:

Sir Gawain and the Green Knight, ed. J.R.R. Tolkien and E.V. Gordon, 2nd edition rev. N. Davis, Oxford 1968

Two Old French Gauvain Romances, ed. R.C. Johnson and D.D.R. Owen, Scottish Academic Press 1972

and also:

L.D. Benson, *Art and Tradition in Sir Gawain and the Green Knight*, New Brunswick, N.J., 1975

L.H. Loomis in *Arthurian Literature in the Middle Ages. A Collaborative History*, ed. R.S. Loomis, Oxford 1959.

ONE

The Feast

*Arthur is unwilling to eat
until something momentous has happened*

It was Pentecost, and the queen was sitting beside King Arthur at the head of the table, and there were a good many counts and kings, dukes and queens and countesses; all the masses had been sung, and the ladies and knights had returned from church. Kay came through the hall, without a coat or mantle, holding a stick in his right hand and wearing a hat of rich cloth upon his fair-haired head. There was not a more handsome knight in all the world, and his hair was plaited in a braid; but his beauty and his prowess were spoiled by his wicked mocking. His tunic was of a rich cloth coloured with a fine, deep dye, and it was girdled with a finely worked belt of which the buckle and all the links were gold: I can say that with confidence, for so the source-book testifies. Everyone stepped out of his path as he strode through the middle of the hall; they all feared his base jests and his evil tongue, and they made way for him. Any wise man fears open spitefulness, whether it be in seriousness or jest. All those present greatly feared his base mockery, and no-one said a word to him. As they all watched, Kay went up to where the king was sitting and said:

'If you wanted, sir, you could eat at once.'

'Kay,' said the king, 'leave me in peace. Never, by the eyes in my head, will I eat on so great a feast-day when I hold so full a court, until some news arrives here.'

From *Perceval*, translated by Nigel Bryant, ed. cit., pp. 30–31.

Arthur keeps Christmas at Carlisle where, before
the celebrations are concluded, an unexpected visitor arrives
with an unwelcome demand

Then afterwards he keeps Christmas at Carlisle, this same famous conqueror, and presides as lord, with dukes and peers from various realms, earls and archbishops and many others – bishops and novices in arms and noble knights of higher rank that flocked to his banner, coming as they pleased. But on Christmas day itself, when they were all assembled, that handsome conqueror himself commanded that every lord should remain and no-one take his leave until full ten days were completely at an end. Thus in royal array he held his Round Table with splendour and delight and exquisite foods. There was never such splendour in living memory, ever before, displayed in midwinter in the western marches. (64–77)

But on New Year's Day, just at noon, as the knights were at table, being served with roast meats, there suddenly came in a senator from Rome with sixteen knights following him in his suite. He greeted the king and then those in the hall, one king after the other, and made his bows. He greeted Guenevere in her place as he saw fit, and afterwards revealed his purpose to the king.

'Sir Lucius Iberius, the Emperor of Rome, greets you as his subject under his noble seal by these credentials, sir king, with angry words. Do not suppose that these are trifles: his arms confirm them. Now, on this New Year's Day, with the seal of the notary, I summon you in this hall to sue for your lands.' (78–91)

Arthur is enraged, but eventually invites the Romans to stay for a week while he takes counsel, and they are duly welcomed:

He orders Sir Kay: 'Take care of these lords and welcome those stern men as their rank demands, so that they are accommodated quickly in the best rooms, and afterwards suitably served in the hall; and in such a way that they find no lack of fodder for their horses, nor of wine, nor of candles, nor of wealth in this land. Do not grudge the spices, but spend what you like so that there is liberality everywhere, and no shortage seen. If you take care of my honour, sir, by my truth you shall have very great treasures that will always avail you.'

Now they are well accommodated within the household, swiftly brought within the high walls by courteous men. They changed their clothes in rooms with fireplaces and then the chancellor with noble chivalry summoned them. Soon the senator was seated, as pleased him well, at the king's own table: two knights served him by himself in fact (as they did Arthur), splendidly on the king's right hand at the Round Table. (156–173)

Then the feast begins:

At the first course there came in before the king himself, boars' heads on bright dishes of burnished silver, with well-trained and experienced servants in fine togas of royal red, all alike, sixty at a time. There was meat served in a sauce with delicious frumenty, as well as choice game, and excellent birds – peacocks and plovers on gold plates, wild porcupines and after them herons in a rich sauce very well disguised, then immediately after, enormous swans on silver dishes, and tarts from Turkey for everyone who liked to taste them. Delicacies were quickly brought in, most delicious to taste, shoulders of wild boar and brawn in slices, geese and bitterns in deep dishes. There were young hawks in pastry that were never bettered, with breasts of pork that looked superb. Then followed various stews with special effects, of blue flames seeming to burn all over them. On every dish the flames burnt up very high, so that everyone who wished to do so could see them. There were cranes and curlews carefully roasted, rabbits in a well-seasoned sauce, and pheasants displayed on polished silver, with gilded pasties and plenty of delicacies. Then there was claret and Cretan wine ingeniously flowing in amazing conduits all of purest silver, sweet wine and Spanish wine and plenty of others – Rhine wine and wine from Rochelle, never finer, excellent strong wine from Venice and Crete from taps of gold for anyone who wished for it. (176–205)

From *Morte Arthure*, ed. Edmund Brock for the Early English Text Society, 1871.

Belshazzar's Feast

Then the floor of the hall was hidden by the number of knights, and barons were ready everywhere at the side-tables, for none was placed upon the dais but the great man himself, and his beautiful concubines in brilliant clothes.

When all the men were seated then the meal began to be served. Harsh trumpets, with broad banners hanging from them, gleaming with gold, struck up their notes in the hall, and their blasts resounded everywhere along the walls; men carrying roast meats on broad dishes of silver in matching style, and soups along with them, lifted little houses cut out of paper, carved on top, and tipped with gold, above the dishes; there were figures of fierce baboons above, animals underneath, birds in artificial foliage fluttering between, and all was richly enamelled in azure and dark blue; the whole device was carried in by men on horseback; and the noise of drums, the music of pipes, tambourines and tabours, sounded one with another – and cymbals and the flourishes of trumpets answered the noise, and the rattle of drumsticks clattered at speed. So the people about the hall were frequently served, with delight at each different course, in the presence of the lord himself, as he and all his loves remained at the table. Wine was brought to him so fast that it warmed his heart, and vapourised into his brain and impaired his judgment, and his mind became weak, and he became almost an idiot; for he looked about and saw his wenches, and his bold barons around the walls.

From *Cleanness*, ed. Sir Israel Gollancz, Cambridge 1974, translated by D.S. Brewer, lines 1397–1424.

The Feast at Cambyuskan's court, in Chaucer's Squire's Tale

This Cambyuskan, of which I have yow toold,
In roial vestiment sit on his deys,
With diademe, ful heighe in his paleys,
And halt his feeste so solempne and so ryche
That in this world ne was ther noon it lyche;
Of which if I shal tellen al th'array,
Thanne wolde it occupie a someres day,

And eek it nedeth nat for to devyse
At every cours the ordre of hire servyse.
I wol nat tellen of hir strange sewes,
Ne of hir swannes, ne of hire heronsewes.
Eek in that lond, as tellen knyghtes olde,
Ther is som mete that is ful deynte holde
That in this lond men recche of it but smal;
Ther nys no man that may reporten al.
I wol nat taryen yow, for it is pryme
And for it is no fruyt but los of tyme;
Unto my firste I wole have my recours.

Chaucer, *The Squire's Tale*, from The Riverside Chaucer, 3rd edition, ed.
Larry D. Benson, Oxford 1987, lines 58–75.

Chaucer's Parson censures 'pride of the table'

Pride of the table appeereth eek ful ofte; for certes, riche men
been cleped to festes, and povre folk been put awey and rebuked.
Also in excesse of diverse metes and drynkes, and namely swich
manere bake-metes and dissh-metes, brennynge of wilde fir and
peynted and castelled with papir, and semblable wast, so that it is
abusioun for to thynke. And eek in to greet preciousnesse of
vessel and curiositee of mynstralcie, by whiche a man is stired the
moore to delices of luxurie, if so be that he sette his herte the lasse
upon oure Lord Jhesu Crist, certeyn it is a synne; and certeinly
the delices myghte been so grete in this caas that man myghte
lightly falle by them into deedly synne.

Chaucer, *The Parson's Tale*, ed. cit. pp. 301–2

TWO

The Beheading Game

The Feast of Bricriu

This contains the earliest recorded version of the beheading game, though the story itself may be much older. The prose narrative, in Middle Irish, is found in a manuscript dating from about 1100. In each of the two quite separate beheading episodes, Cuchulainn is the hero, but there are nevertheless a number of similarities with the story of *Sir Gawain and the Green Knight*.

A big powerful fellow was Terror, son of Great Fear. He used to shift his form into what shape he pleased, was wont to do tricks of magic and such like arts. He in sooth was the wizard from whom Muni, the Wizard's Pass, is named. He used to be called 'wizard' from the extent to which he changed his divers shapes.

To Terror at his loch they accordingly went. Yellow had given them a guide. To Terror they told the cause for which they had sought him out. He said he should venture on adjudgement provided only they would adhere to it.

'We will adhere to it,' they said; whereupon he solemnly pledges them.

'I have a covenant to make with you,' he said, 'and whoever of you fulfills it with me, he is the man who wins the Champion's Portion.'

'What is the covenant?' they said.

'I have an axe, and the man into whose hands it shall be put is to cut off my head today, I to cut off his tomorrow.'

Thereupon Conall and Loigaire said they would not agree to that arrangement, for it would be impossible for them to live after having been beheaded, although he might. Therefore they

18

declined (shirked) that: [although other books narrate that they agreed to the bargain, to wit, Loigaire to cut off Terror's (Uath's) head the first day, and (on the giant's returning) that Loigaire shirked his part of the bargain and that Conall likewise behaved unfairly]. Cuchulainn, however, said he would agree to the covenant (bargain) were the Champion's Portion given to him. Conall and Loigaire said they would allow him that, if he agreed to a wager with Terror. Cuchulainn solemnly pledged them not to contest the Champion's Portion if he made covenant with Terror. And they then pledged him to ratify it. Terror, having put spells on the edge of the axe, lays his head upon the stone for Cuchulainn. Cuchulainn with his own axe gives the giant a blow and cuts off his head. He then went off from them into the loch, his axe and his head on his breast.

On the morrow he comes back on his quest. Cuchulainn stretches himself out for him on the stone. The axe with its edge reversed he draws down thrice on Cuchulainn's neck.

'Get up,' said Terror; 'the sovranty of the heroes of Erin to Cuchulainn, and the Champion's Portion without contest.'

The three heroes then went to Emain. But Loigaire and Conall disputed the verdict given in favour of Cuchulainn and the original contest as to the Champion's Portion continued. The Ultonians advised them to go for judgement to Curoi. To that too they agreed.

The Champion's Covenant

Once upon a time, as the Ultonians were in Emain, fatigued after the gathering and the games, Conchobar and Fergus mac Roig, with Ultonia's nobles as well, proceeded from the sporting field outside and sat in the Royal Court (lit. Red Branch) of Conchobar. Neither Cuchulainn nor Conall the Victorious nor Loigaire the Triumphant were there that night. But the hosts of Ultonia's valiant heroes were there. As they were seated, it being eventide, and the day drawing towards a close, they saw a big uncouth fellow of exceeding ugliness drawing nigh them into the hall. To them it seemed as if none of the Ultonians would reach half his height. Horrible and ugly was the carl's guise. Next his skin he wore an old hide with a dark dun mantle around him, and over him a great spreading club-tree (branch) the size of a winter-shed, under which thirty bullocks could find shelter. Ravenous yellow eyes he had, protruding from his head, each of the twain the size of an ox-vat. Each finger as thick as another person's wrist. In his left hand a stock, a burden for twenty yoke of oxen. In his right hand an axe weighing thrice fifty glowing molten masses [of metal]. Its handle would require a plough-team (a yoke of six) to move it. Its sharpness such that it would lop off hairs, the wind blowing them against its edge.

In that guise he went and stood by the fork-beam beside the fire.

'Is the hall lacking in room for you,' quoth Duach of the Chafer Tongue to the uncouth clodhopper, 'that ye find no other place than by the fork-beam, unless ye wish to be domestic luminary? – only sooner will a blaze be to the house than brightness to the household.'

'What property soever may be mine, sooth ye will agree, no matter how big I am, that the household as a whole will be enlightened, while the hall will not be burnt.

'That, however, is not my sole function; I have others as well. But neither in Erin nor in Alba nor in Europe nor in Africa nor in Asia, including Greece, Scythia, the Isles of Gades, the Pillars of Hercules, and Bregon's Tower (Brigantium), have I found the quest on which I have come, nor a man to do me fair play regarding it. Since ye Ultonians have excelled all the folks of those lands in strength, prowess, valour; in rank, magnanimity, dignity; in truth, generosity and worth, get ye one among you to give me the boon I crave.'

'In sooth it is not just that the honour of a province is to be carried off,' said Fergus mac Roich, 'because of one man who fails to keep his word of honour. Death, certainly, is not a whit nearer to him than to you.'

'Not that I shun it,' quoth he.

'Make thy quest known to us then,' quoth Fergus mac Roich.

'If but fair play be vouchsafed me, I will tell it.'

'It is right also to give fair play,' quoth Sencha, son of Ailill, 'for it beseemeth not a great clannish folk to break a mutual covenant over any unknown individual. To us too it seemeth likely, if at long last you find such a person, you will find here one worthy of you.'

'Conchobar I put aside,' he quoth, 'for sake of his sovranty, and Fergus mac Roich also on account of his like privilege. These two excepted, come whosoever of you that may venture, that I may cut off his head tonight, he mine tomorrow night.'

'Sure then there is no warrior here,' said Duach, 'after these two.'

'By my troth there will be this moment,' quoth Fat-Neck, son of Short Neck, as he sprang on to the floor of the hall.

The strength then of yon Fat-Neck was as the strength of a hundred warriors, each arm having the might of a hundred centaurs.

'Bend down, bachlach,' said Fat-Neck, 'that I may cut your head off tonight, you to cut off mine tomorrow night.'

'Were that my quest, I could have got it anywhere,' said the bachlach. 'Let us act according to our covenant,' he said, 'I to cut off your head tonight, you to avenge it tomorrow night.'

'By my people's god,' quoth Duach of the Chafer Tongue, 'death is thus for thee no pleasant prospect should the man killed tonight attack thee on the morrow. It is given to you alone if you have the power, being killed night after night (*lit.* to be killed every night), to avenge it next day.'

'Truly I will carry out what you all as a body agree upon by way of counsel, strange as it may seem to you,' said the bachlach.

He then pledged the other to keep his troth in this contention as to fulfilling his tryst on the morrow.

With that Fat-Neck took the axe from out of the bachlach's hand. Seven feet apart were its two angles. Then did the bachlach put his neck across the block. Fat-Neck dealt a blow across it with the axe till it stuck in the block underneath, cutting off the head till it lay by the base of the fork-beam, the house being filled with the blood. Straightway the bachlach rose, recovered himself, clasped his head, block and axe to his breast, thus made his exit from the hall with blood streaming from his neck. It filled the Red Branch on every side. Great was the folk's horror, wondering at the marvel that had appeared to them.

'By my people's god,' said Duach of the Chafer Tongue, 'if the bachlach, having been killed tonight, come back tomorrow, he will not leave a man alive in Ultonia.'

The following night, however, he returned, and Fat-Neck shirked him. Then began the bachlach to urge his pact with Fat-Neck.

'Sooth it is not right for Fat-Neck not to fulfil his covenant with me.'

That night, however, Loigaire the Triumphant was present.

'Who of the warriors that contest Ultonia's Champion's Portion will carry out a covenant tonight with me? Where is Loigaire the Triumphant?' quoth he.

'Here,' said Loigaire.

He pledged him too, yet Loigaire kept not his tryst. The bachlach returned on the morrow and similarly pledged Conall Cernach, who came not as he had sworn.

The fourth night the bachlach returned, and fierce and furious was he. All the ladies came that night to see the strange marvel that had come into the Red Branch. That night Cuchulainn was there also. Then the fellow began to upbraid them.

'Ye men of Ultonia, your valour and your prowess are gone. Your warriors greatly covet the Champion's Portion, yet are unable to contest it. Where is yon poor mad wight that is hight Cuchulainn? Fain would I know if *his* word be better than the others'.'

'No covenant do I desire with you,' said Cuchulainn.

'Likely is that, you wretched fly; greatly thou dost fear to die.'

Whereupon Cuchulainn sprang towards him and dealt him a blow with the axe, hurling his head to the top rafter of the Red Branch till the whole hall shook. Cuchulainn again caught up the head and gave it a blow with the axe and smashed it. Thereafter the bachlach rose up.

On the morrow the Ultonians were watching Cuchulainn to see whether he would shirk the bachlach as the other heroes had done. As Cuchulainn was awaiting the bachlach, they saw that great dejection seized him. It had been fitting had they sung his dirge. They felt sure his life would last only till the bachlach came. Then quoth Cuchulainn with shame to Conchobar:

'Thou shall not go until my pledge to the bachlach is fulfilled; for death awaits me, and I would rather have death with honour.'

They were there as the day was closing when they saw the bachlach approaching.

'Where is Cuchulainn?' he said.

'Here am I,' he answered.

'You're dull of speech tonight, unhappy one; greatly you fear to die. Yet, though great your fear, death you have not shirked.'

Thereafter Cuchulainn went up to him and stretched his neck across the block, which was of such size that his neck reached but half-way.

'Stretch out your neck, you wretch,' the bachlach said.

'You keep me in torment,' quoth Cuchulainn. 'Despatch me quickly; last night, by my troth, I tormented you not. Verily I swear if you torment me, I shall make myself as long as a crane above you.'

'I cannot slay you,' quoth the bachlach, 'what with the size of the block and the shortness of your neck and of your side.'

Then Cuchulainn stretched out his neck so that a warrior's full-grown foot would have fitted between any two of his ribs; his neck he distended till it reached the other side of the block. The bachlach raised his axe till it reached the roof-tree of the hall. The creaking of the old hide that was about the fellow and the crashing of the axe – both his arms being raised aloft with all his might – were as the loud noise of a wood tempest-tossed in a night of storm. Down it came then . . . on his neck, its blunt side below, – all the nobles of Ultonia gazing upon them.

'O Cuchulainn, arise! . . . Of the warriors of Ultonia and Erin, no matter their mettle, none is found to be compared with thee in valour, bravery and truthfulness. The sovranty of the heroes of Erin to thee from this hour forth and the Champion's Portion undisputed, and to thy lady the precedence alway of the ladies of Ultonia in the Mead Hall. And whosoever shall lay wager against thee from now, as my folks swear I swear, while on life he will be in sore scathe.'

Then the bachlach vanished. It was Curoi mac Dairi who in that guise had come to fulfil the promise he had given to Cuchulainn.

From *Fled Bricrend. The Feast of Bricriu*, ed. and tr. George Henderson, Irish Text Society II, London 1899. By permission of the Irish Text Society.

The Story of Carados

Chrétien de Troyes did not live to finish his story of Perceval. But after his death other story-tellers took up the tale in order to explain what happened to Chrétien's characters. The first Continuator (there appear to have been four quite different ones) continued the story in his own way and added a separate romance – the Carados story – to the tale.[1]

It has been suggested that the version of the beheading game with which the story of Carados deals was probably familiar to the first Continuator, not directly from *Fled Bricrend* itself, but through intermediary versions, now lost, probably by Breton jongleurs.[2]

Of this *first* Continuation, with its account of Carados, there were different forms or redactions. The story was thus retold in a number of quite different MSS, which gave basically similar accounts but with some variation in the details. I have included passages from two of these redactions, the Mixed and the Long, omitting the Short, which is very similar to the Mixed. Of the three, the Long Redaction seems to be closest in detail to *Sir Gawain and the Green Knight*.

The story of Carados evidently continued to be very popular, however, for in 1530 a prose version was produced in Paris from an older metrical version. I have also included the portion of this which deals with the beheading game. It shows (as do the later English versions of *Sir Gawain and the Green Knight*) how popular stories were handed down over long periods of time, gathering new elements as they went, sometimes appearing to gain in strength, as the redactions of *Carados* do, sometimes declining, as the versions of *Sir Gawain and the Green Knight* do.

---

[1] W. Roach, in *Continuations of the Old French Perceval*, Philadelphia, 1949–55.
[2] L.D. Benson in *Art and Tradition in Sir Gawain and the Green Knight*, New Brunswick 1955.

From The Story of Carados – First Version

And as Arthur was thus speaking, and the others were holding their peace, they saw a very big knight come through the door of the palace on a warhorse with white hooves. He was dressed in an ermine robe which almost swept the ground. He had on his head a coronet with a golden circlet upon the cloth, and was girded with a long sword which had a hilt of pure gold, and the sword-belt was edged with gold. So he came on the horse right up to the dais and said very loudly in the hearing of all:

'King Arthur, may God who does not lie grant you honour and long life.'

'Friend, may he bless you.'

'King,' said he, 'I ask you a boon.'

'Knight, name it at once, and what can be, you shall have.'

And he replied:

'You shall know it: to give a sword-blow without deception, asking another to be received of you.'

'Friend, what is that? What are you saying?'

'King, I say to you that without the least doubt, if there is a knight here who can cut my head off with a single blow with this sword, and I can after the blow recover my health and strength, he can be sure to have without fail, a year from today, a similar blow in exchange, if he dares wait for it.'

Then without another word he dismounted. He drew his sword and so held it out to them, but there was no-one there who dared take it. But all the knights said that whoever did would be extremely foolish, for by it he would run into danger, and thus he would have neither reward nor honour.

'Ha, lord!' said the knight, 'Is that it? No striking with it? Now you can see, King Arthur, that your court is not so noble as everyone says and swears; there is not a single bold knight there. I testify to you truly, and I say that in future tales will be told about it everywhere that are not at all pretty.'

He was just on the point of going when Carados who was a new knight sprang forward. So he prepared himself for this great exploit and threw his cloak to the ground, whoever he might displease, or whoever might be pleased. He came to him, took the sword and drew it out in his right hand. The king saw it, much distressed by it, and said:

'Good nephew, you can relinquish this exploit without shame. There is many a good knight here who can strike as well or better than you, if they wished to do it. They are dumbfounded because the undertaking is so very foolish.'

When Carados heard the king, he felt such shame that he was all red. Not on that account did he wish to give up, so he came close to the knight. In order to strike better he grasped the sword firmly, and the knight turned towards the king, lowered his head, and stretched out his neck. Carados struck so vigorously that he made the head fly towards the dais, but the knight took it by the hair in his two hands just as if he was quite whole. So he joined it on again immediately.

'Carados,' he said, 'you have struck me.'

'Truly,' said Kay, 'and little good has it done you. A year from today, however it will turn out, you will not wish to be set in his place, to possess the whole of this country.'

'Carados,' said the knight, 'a year from today, dear good friend, I shall be back here, you may be sure; so do not fail for anything, or not be found here at the right time.'

Then he went off, he stayed there no longer; and the king was very angry and very sad, and he greatly lamented. So did the other knights; they scarcely wanted to eat, they were so angry and downcast. The court broke up with great grief; together they all went back to the lands where they were before. But first the king gave his orders that a year later each one should come, and the gathering be at Carlisle again. And the story of Carados soon reached the king, his father, and the queen, his mother, who were filled with great grief and anger. But of him I can truly say to you, that he was so carefree and so joyous that there was no man living in this world who could perceive from his appearance that he was at all afraid; so he went seeking exploits and hard feats of chivalry. Thus the year was completed, to the day which was appointed and set. His father did not wish to come because he could not see him die, nor the mother who had borne him.

The court reassembled at Carlisle at Pentecost, at the palace – a court so great that there were many people who had never been there before, for insomuch as the king had power, he did not allow any knight to stay away and not come to that feast, where Carados was to lose his head in the sight of the king and his barons. After the great processions and after the solemn mass, the noble barons brought in the king to his palace again, but he had a very sorrowful expression and so had all the others all the time. As soon as they were seated in silence the knight came in through the door – bringing the evil present, he immediately opened the door. He came on horseback, armed with a sword, into the decorated room, to the high table where the king was sitting. Without saying a word he dismounted, drew his sword, took the naked blade, and said in Arthur's hearing:

'Carados, come here. Where are you?'

'You can see I'm here,' said Carados.

'Then come forward,' said the knight.

Willingly Carados removed his cloak and immediately came to the spot where he saw the other standing, making a great show of being angry. The king saw him, greatly grieving, but he was never slow to speak.

'Ha, knight!' he said. 'Have mercy on my nephew; do not kill him. You shall have as great a ransom as you know how to devise.'

'Say what, then.'

'You can have all the armour and the churls and the nobles in this court. Never before has anyone been offered so great a ransom.'

'King, that is not much. Can I have more?'

'Yes,' he said, 'all the treasure and the vessels of silver and gold which have been brought here.'

'King,' said he, 'that will be nothing, because however much treasure there is in the world, or there ever will be, I would not take it in exchange for him.'

When the king heard it, he grieved exceedingly, and the others too, on every side.

'Knight, you are a great coward,' said Carados. 'Do immediately what you have to do.'

And he reached out his arm and lifted his sword on high as if he intended to strike a great blow. The king now fainted, and the queen came out weeping from her rooms when she heard the news, and the ladies and girls too. When she saw the naked sword all the blood left her face and fled from it; she was deeply anguished and grieved. She came towards him as one who was not slow and said to him:

'Leave off, knight, a little while. Dear good sir, do not kill him. Instead of him you can have a mistress – lady or girl, whoever she may be – from among the most beautiful here, or else all of them if it pleases you.'

'Lady queen, that is nothing. I will not take all the ladies in the world in exchange for his head, nor all the girls that are here. Go away quickly into your rooms, my dear lady, and pray to God for his soul, that He will send it to paradise.'

The queen covered her face and so turned away weeping, and the others followed her wailing. The knight raised the sword: he threatened to strike a great blow. At that, most of those in the palace fell fainting all in a heap. But he had not the intention of striking, so he took Carados gently by the hand and said:

'Carados, get up. I will not do you any more harm now because you are too valiant a knight, and strong and trustworthy and proud. But come here, and speak to me in private.'

Far away from the king he led him, over to one side, and said:

'You are my son, may God preserve me!'

From *Continuations of the Old French Perceval*, ed. W. Roach and R.H. Ivy, Jr., Philadelphia 1949–55.
The First Continuation, Vol. I, lines 3332–3544 (MSS T V D) (The Mixed Redaction)

From The Story of Carados – Second Version

Just as they were speaking, lo and behold a knight on a grey
horse appeared at the doorway. He had ridden his horse at great
speed, and came singing a song. He had a hat on his head
because of the great heat, and was clad in a robe of ermine over
which he had girded a sword, adorned with a tassel of fine silk,
with which to cut off his head. He stopped right before the king
and said:

'King, God save you! I am come to ask a boon of you as the best
and highest king on earth, if you please to grant it to me.'

'Friend,' said the king, 'you are welcome. Your greeting is
returned to you. When I have heard the boon that you wish to ask
of me, know this, that I shall never fail you.'

'King,' said he, 'I do not wish to deceive you. The boon is to
receive a blow for another blow given.'

'What? I must get this clear.'

'King, I shall explain it to you. I shall make the gift of this sword
to a knight here before your eyes. If he can cut off my head in one
stroke, it is up to him! If I can then recover from the blow, grant
me a blow in return in a year from today, here before you.'

'By St John,' said Kay, 'I shall not strike for all the wealth in
Normandy. Sir knight, he would be a fool who would strike here
on such terms.'

The knight dismounted.

'King,' he said, 'if you have denied me the boon I wish to ask of
you, it will be talked about by everyone. Indeed, you could be
sure that it was true to say that you would have failed your court
on account of this little boon that I request, coming as a stranger
from a distance to ask you.'

He drew his sword from his scabbard. The king had a
thoughtful look, and both the great and the lowly were taken
aback. In their hearts they thought of the honour they might gain
by striking him. Carados, who was a new knight, could not bear it
any longer. He threw his cloak down and ran to the knight. He
took the weapon of steel in his hand. The knight spoke one of his
characteristic sayings to him:

'Are you chosen as the best?'

'Certainly not! But as the most foolish.'

The knight extended his neck and put his head on the table. You may be sure that the king was very angry, and all the barons in the court. Sir Yvain all but ran to snatch the sword from his hands, but still it was only the desire of an instant, for he could not take it from him. Carados raised the sword and gave him such a blow that he cut almost through the table. The head flew far away, but the body followed it so close that as one looked it was caught, and the body snatched back the head and replaced it in its right place. The knight jumped into the middle, all safe and sound before the king.

'King,' he said, 'do not fail me. As I have received this blow in your court, I shall be back to have my own in a year from today.'

The king made no more delay; immediately the barons agreed, and all the rest both high and low, that just as they were now at his court, so they would be on this particular day the next year, in that same place.

'Carados,' the knight said, 'you have given me a great blow before the king. In a year from today you will have mine in return.'

Then he went on his way. The knight left the court and the king remained full of anger because his mind was obsessed with this business. No-one could assuage the grief that the knights and the ladies expressed; they had scarcely the heart to eat, and all the court was distressed. Carados was not upset, and he said:

'Uncle, let me leave here, for it is all in God's hands.'

Many an eye wept for Carados. The court was summoned to Carlisle at Pentecost the next year. The King of Vame and Lady Ysave his wife heard the news which cost Carados so much. They expressed so very great a grief for their beloved child that no-one could describe or relate the great sorrow and the agony that they experienced all through the year. And Carados remained at the court of his uncle the king. He did not take thought for his life but went to seek for adventures. Never did you hear, in all your life, of a single knight continually doing so many chivalrous deeds as he did that year. He was spoken of in many places that year, and everyone who saw him grieved and wept that the head of such a one should not remain longer. They had to assemble at the court, and all those who heard tell of it came by land and by sea to see the marvel, with many a girl and many a lady. King Carados [of Vame] and his wife were so grief-stricken that they did not dare to come, but you may be sure that they did not rest. They made many offerings and gifts for Carados on that occasion, that God who is over all good things might defend him from shame that day. It was the day of Pentecost. The adventure that he much dreaded weighed heavily on Carados and was painful for him to think about. The court was all assembled, and the processions went off, the masses in the chapels were sung, and the water was proffered before the meal. Then lo and behold! a knight on his horse, girded with a sword, a knight who did not have a pale complexion, but was red with the heat.

'Sir king,' he said, 'may God save you.'

'Friend, may God bless you too.'

'Carados, I do not see you. Come forward, and thus you will have your feast. Offer me your head here, because I put mine there for you before, so it is quite right that I should see once more how I can strike with the sword; and so you will receive your blow.'

Carados saw and understood clearly that it was now time for him to act. He stripped himself and sprang forward. He offered his head to the knight and said to him:

'Good sir, now you have me; do the best you can.'

'Sir knight,' said the king, 'do not be so little courteous as not to take a ransom.'

'Ransom? Tell me what you will give me.'

'I will gladly tell you it; for I will give you a great ransom. I will give you, and I do not lie, as many vessels as can be found in the court, as ever can be brought in, and the armour of a knight, because this is my nephew who is most dear to me.'

'I shall certainly not take it, but I shall take his head straight away. Let him make no defence.'

'But I will say more: I will give you all the treasure, whether precious stones, silver or gold, which can be found in my realms, in Brittany or in England or anywhere in my domain.'

'I certainly will not accept it, but I am going to cut off his head now. You undoubtedly consider me a mere beast, but I will have it this very moment. It cannot escape me, the head – so let him make no defence.'

'I must say one more word to you – '

But he raised the blade and got ready to strike. The king saw it and swooned with grief. Carados said to him in anger:

'Why don't you strike, sir? You make me die twice. If you make such calculations for a blow I shall strongly suspect that you are a coward.'

The queen came to beg for his life from another part of the castle. She came out of her room, and with her came many hundreds of ladies and girls who were extremely beautiful.

'Sir knight, don't touch him,' she said. 'It would be a sin and a pity if he were to be killed. Have mercy on him for God's sake. When you have given me his death you will be well rewarded. Take advice, if you would act well. Will you do nothing for me? Delay an hour for me: you claim requital for the blow of Carados the king's nephew, for whom a great ransom will be given. See all these young women and beautiful girls with graceful bodies: you can have them all. Leave off, if you would act wisely.'

'Lady,' the knight replied, 'I certainly could not take so many ladies in this world, nor any other living pledge. If you cannot bear to look, go and stay in your room.'

The queen covered her head and her grief broke out again. She went into her room with the ladies of the land, and all together made great lamentation because Carados was so close to death. The king and all those knights did not know what to advise, so they gave vent to grief such that no mortal man could have restrained it. Carados moved towards a table and laid his head down on it, and the other raised the sword and struck him with the flat but did not hurt him at all.

'Carados,' he said, 'get up now, for it will be too great an outrage and a very great pity if I kill you. Come and speak to me over here: I want to give you a little advice.'

He spoke these words to him in private:

'Do you know why I haven't killed you? You are my son, and I am your father.'

From *Continuations of the Old French Perceval*, ed. W. Roach and R.H. Ivy, Jr., Philadelphia 1949-55.
The First Continuation, vol. II, p. 210, lines 7137-7383 (MSS E M Q U) (The Long Redaction)

Sir Gawain and the Haughty Maiden

After being welcomed at a castle, Gawain visits the chapel with the lady and finds himself in danger of being beheaded.

. . . Sir Gawain rode on until, deep in the forest, he came upon a most handsome and splendid castle. Out of the castle an aged knight had ridden to hunt, with a hawk perched on his wrist. He greeted Sir Gawain, who returned the greeting and asked the name of the fine castle he could see. It was the castle, said the knight, of the Haughty Maiden, who never deigned to ask any knight his name. 'And we who are in her service dare not ask on her behalf. But you shall be well lodged at the castle, for in other ways she is a most gracious lady, and the most beautiful in all the land. She has never had a husband, nor ever deigned to love a knight unless she heard that he was the finest knight in the world. But come, I will accompany you on your way.'

'Great thanks,' said Sir Gawain.

They rode into the castle together, and dismounted at the steps of the great hall. The knight took Sir Gawain by the hand and led him upstairs to be stripped of his arms, and brought him a coat of rich scarlet cloth, all lined with fur, which he fastened for him. Then he brought the lady of the castle to greet Sir Gawain, who rose as she came and said:

'My lady, may good fortune ever follow you!'

'I bid you welcome, sir knight,' she said, and taking him by the hand she led him into the castle chambers.

'Would you like to see my chapel, sire?' she said.

'As you like, damsel,' said Sir Gawain, and she led him there.

Gawain looked about him and thought he had never entered a chapel so beautiful or so richly adorned. There before him were four tombs, the finest he had ever seen, and all were covered; and on the right-hand side of the chapel were three recesses in the wall, all set about with gold and precious stones, at the back of which could be seen the bright gleam of candles, with crosses and amulets, and they smelt sweeter than balsam.

'Sire,' said the maiden, 'do you see those tombs?'

'Yes, damsel.'

'Three of them, sire, have been made for the three finest knights in the world, and the fourth one is for me. One of the knights is named Gawain, and another is Lancelot of the Lake, and each of them I love deeply; but the third, whose name is Perceval, I love more than either of them. In those three recesses which you can see, relics have been placed out of love for them. But look; I will show you what I would do to them if they were here – and if I cannot do it to the three together, I shall do it to one or two of them.'

She reached towards the recesses and pulled on a golden bolt which was fixed in the wall, and thereupon a steel blade, sharper than a razor, crashed down and closed the three holes.

'Thus will I cut off their heads when they go to worship the relics in the recesses. Then I shall take their bodies and place them in these tombs with much honour, richly shrouded. For I can have no joy of them while they are alive, but joy I shall have of them dead; and when it shall please God that I die, I shall be laid to rest in the fourth coffin in the company of the three good knights.'

Sir Gawain heard all this and wondered much, wishing that the night were already over. Then they left the chapel; and that night the maiden did Sir Gawain much honour. She had a great company of knights to serve her and to help her defend the castle, and they honoured Gawain most highly, though they did not know that it was he, and no-one asked his name for that was not the custom of the castle. But the maiden knew that the three knights often rode through the forest, and she had given orders to four of her knights who guarded the forest and its paths to bring to her any of the three, if they should pass by, and she would reward them by enlarging their fiefs.

Sir Gawain stayed in the castle that night, and the next morning he went to hear mass before departing. After mass he armed himself and took his leave of the maiden and her knights, and galloped out of the castle with no pressing desire to return. Into the deep forest he went, and had ridden a full league when he came upon two knights sitting in a defile. As soon as they saw him coming they leapt on to their horses, fully armed, and with shields hung from their necks and lances in hand they came to meet him.

'Halt there, sir knight,' they cried, 'and tell us your name in all truthfulness.'

'Gladly, my lords,' he said. 'I have never kept my name from anyone who asked it. My name is Gawain, the nephew of King Arthur.'

'Oh, you are welcome, sire!' they said. 'We wished for nothing more. Come with us to the lady on the hill, who is most anxious to see you, and will receive you with joy at the Proud Castle where she resides.'

From *The High Book of The Grail: A translation of the 13th century romance of Perlesvaus* by Nigel Bryant, ed. cit., pp. 54–6.

The Story of Lancelot in the Waste Land

Lancelot comes to a city which has been laid waste, where he beheads a young knight, returning a year later for a return blow.

Then Lancelot left the Hermitage, and rode until he came out of the forest and found a waste land, and a vast and extensive countryside, where there were neither beasts nor birds, because the land was so dry and so poor that they could find no pasture. Lancelot looked ahead into the distance and saw a city appear, so he rode at great speed in that direction, and saw that the city was so large that it seemed to extend over an entire region. He saw that the walls were falling down all around, and the gates sagging with age. He went in and found the city quite empty of people, and saw great palaces fallen and devastated, and found the markets and the exchanges all empty and saw great burial-grounds all full of tombs, and the churches all laid waste. He rode through the broad streets and came upon a great palace which seemed to be finer and more intact than all the others. He stopped before it, and heard and listened how the knights and ladies kept up a great lament, and they said to the knight:

'Alas, what great griefs and what great wrongs are come upon you, that you should have to die in such a manner, so that you cannot avert your death. We are bound to greatly hate him, by whom you are condemned.'

The knights and the ladies fainted at his departure. Lancelot heard all this and was greatly astonished, but he could see nothing. Then, look! the knight is coming down into the hall, dressed in a red tunic, girded with a rich belt of silk and gold, and with a very rich brooch at his neck with very rich stones in it, with a golden cap on his head, and holding a huge axe in his two hands. The knight was very handsome and very young. Lancelot saw him come, and looked on him very gladly, for he saw him quite clearly. And he said to Lancelot:

'Sir, dismount.'

'Willingly, sir,' said Lancelot. He dismounted and tethered his horse to a silver ring which was in the mounting-block, and removed his shield from his neck and his lance from his hand.

'Sir,' he said to the knight, 'What is your wish?'

'Sir,' the knight said to him, 'you must cut off my head with this axe because my death has been appointed with this weapon; or else I shall cut off yours.'

'Indeed, sir;' said Lancelot, 'what did you say?'

'You heard me, sir' said the knight. 'You must do it, since you have come to this city.'

'Sir,' said Lancelot, 'it would be very foolish for one who is in jeopardy not to take what is most to his advantage, but I shall be blamed if I slay you without a fault.'

'I assure you,' said the knight, 'unless you do, you cannot go away.'

'Good sir,' said Lancelot, 'you are so noble and so trusty, how is it that you come so willingly to your death? You well know that I shall kill you before you can kill me since that is how it is.'

'All this I know to be true,' said the knight, 'but you must promise me before I die that you will return to this city in a year's time, and that you will put your head in the same jeopardy as I put mine in now, without resistance.'

'By my own head,' said Lancelot, 'I need no more persuading to choose respite from death rather than to die immediately. But I greatly marvel that you are so well disposed to receive your death.'

'Sir,' said the knight, 'the man who wishes to go before the Saviour of the World ought to purge himself well of all his misdeeds and sins that he has ever committed, and I am truly repentant, so that I wish to die at this moment.'

Then he held out the axe. Lancelot took it and saw that it was very keen and well-sharpened.

'Sir,' said the knight, 'hold out your hand towards that church that you see.'

'Willingly, sir,' said Lancelot.

'Will you swear to me here on the relics of that church,' said the knight, 'that you, in one year from today, at the hour at which you have killed me, or before, will return here and put your head in the same jeopardy as I place mine in, without default?'

'I swear to you here,' said Lancelot.

Then the knight knelt and stretched his neck out as far as he could, and Lancelot took the axe in his two hands and said to him,

'Sir knight, for God's sake, have mercy on yourself.'

'Willingly, sir,' said the knight. 'Just cut off my head; otherwise I cannot have mercy on you.'

'Such mercy I wish I could refuse you,' said Lancelot.

Then he held out the axe and cut off his head with so great a flourish that he made it fly seven feet beyond the body. He fell to the ground when his head was cut off, and Lancelot threw the axe to the ground, thinking that he would do ill to remain there. He came to his horse, took his arms, and mounted; and looking behind, saw neither the body nor the head of the knight, nor did he know what had become of them, except that he heard a great lamentation and a great outcry far off in the city, from the knights and ladies; and they grieved for the good knight, and said that he would be avenged, if God willed, at the appointed time, or before. Lancelot went out of the city; he had heard and understood all that the knights and the ladies had said . . .

King Arthur went out, and Sir Gawain and Sir Lancelot with him. They traversed many strange lands. They entered a great forest. The day was fine and bright, as the sun shone on the shields from time to time. Lancelot remembered the knight that he had killed in the Waste City, to which he had to return, and knew well that the day for his return was approaching. So he told it all to King Arthur, and said that if he did not go he would break his word. They rode until they came to a cross where the ways forked, and stretched away into the forest.

'Sir,' said Lancelot, 'I must go so as to fulfil my pledge, in adventure and in great peril of death; and I do not know that I shall ever see you again because I killed a knight, for which I am full of grief. I had to swear, before I killed him, that I would return to put my head in the same jeopardy as he had put his. Now the day is approaching when I must return; I do not wish to fail in my agreement, because I should be blamed for it. And if God allows me to escape alive, I shall follow you swiftly to the land where you are going.'

The king embraced and kissed him at his departure, and so did Sir Gawain, and prayed the Saviour of the World that He would preserve his body and his life so that they could see him soon. Lancelot would willingly have sent the queen a greeting if had dared, because she was closer to his heart than any other thing; but he did not wish that the king or Sir Gawain should know anything of his love, lest they should be angry. Love was so rooted in his heart, that whatever peril he might enter into, he could not uproot it, and so he devoutly prayed to God every day, to give guidance to the queen, and to deliver him from this great danger so that he might see her again. He rode on so that he came to the Waste City just at mid-day, and found the city as deserted as the first time that he was there . . .

In the city where Lancelot had now arrived there were a large number of ruined churches and many rich palaces which had fallen down, and many great empty halls. He had only just come within the city when he heard a great outcry and lamentation of ladies and young girls, but he did not know from which side it came. They called out all together,

'Ah, God! how the knight who killed the knight here has betrayed us, for he has not returned. Now is the day come for him to fulfill his pledge. Never again can we trust in a knight, since this one has not returned. The others before him have failed us; this one will do the same as the others for fear of death, for he cut off the head of the fairest and best knight who ever lived in this kingdom, so he ought to have his cut off likewise. But he has taken good care not to.'

This is what the ladies said. Lancelot heard them very clearly, and wondered where they were, for he could not see any of them; and he came up to the palace where he had killed the knight. He dismounted, then tied up his horse to a ring which was attached to a marble mounting-block. He had only just done this when a knight came down from the palace, huge and handsome and strong and supple. He was dressed in a short tunic of silk and held in his hand the axe with which Lancelot had cut off the head of the other knight. He came to him sharpening it on a whetstone, so as to cut better. Lancelot saw him coming, and asked him,

'Good sir, what are you doing with that axe?'

'By my head,' said the knight, 'you will find out in the same way as my brother found out.'

'What,' said Lancelot, 'you are going to kill me, then?'

'You will find that out,' said the knight, 'before you leave here. But did you not promise that you would put your head in jeopardy, as the knight whom you killed put his? It was on that condition that you were able to depart. But come on and kneel down, and stretch out your neck so that I can cut off your head. If you do not wish to do it of your own free will, you will soon find that someone will compel you to, even if you were twenty knights. But I know very well that you have not returned for any other reason but to fulfil your pledge, and that you will not argue about it.'

Lancelot thought that he was going to die, and wished to perform without fail what he had promised. He lay down on the ground stretching out his arms in the shape of the cross, and prayed to God to have mercy. He remembered the queen.

'Ah, madam!' he said, 'I shall never see you again. If I could have seen you once before I die, it would have been a great comfort to me, and my soul would have departed more gladly; but that I shall never see you again grieves me more than death itself. To die is fitting when one has lived so long, and I firmly promise you that my love will never fail you, and that my soul will love you as much in the next world as my body does in this, if it has the power.'

Then the tears fell from his eyes; and not from the time when he was first a knight, so the story says, did he shed tears out of sorrow, except for this time and one other. He took three blades of grass, and so gave himself communion. After he had crossed and blessed himself, he got up and knelt down and stretched out his neck. The knight raised the axe. Lancelot heard the blow coming, so lowered his head, and the axe went past him. The knight said to him,

'Sir knight, my brother whom you killed did not do that, but held his head and his neck quite still. And so you ought to do.'

Then two extremely beautiful ladies appeared at the windows of the palace, and recognised Lancelot at once. So when the knight had reached out for another blow, one of the ladies called out,

'If you wish to have my love for evermore, throw down the axe, and call the knight quits. Otherwise, you will lose my love for ever.'

The knight immediately threw the axe down on the ground and falling at Lancelot's feet, begged mercy of him as the truest knight in the world.

'But you should have mercy on me and not kill me,' said Lancelot.

'Sir,' he replied, 'I shall not kill you; instead, I shall help you against everyone in the world, although you have killed my brother.'

The ladies came down from the palace and towards Lancelot.

'Sir,' they said, 'we ought to love you more than anyone else in the world, because we are the two sisters that you saw so poor in the Waste Castle, where you stayed with our brother, you and Sir Gawain and another knight, to whom you gave the treasure and the fortress of the robber knights that you killed. This city which is waste and the Waste Castle of my brother would never again be filled with people, nor should we ever have had our lands again, if a knight as noble as you had not come. At least twenty knights have come here in the same way as you came; each one killed a brother or uncle or cousin of ours, and cut off his head as you did that of the knight; and each one promised that he would return on the day to be appointed. Every one broke the covenant, because not one of them dared to return there. And if you, like the others, had failed to return on the day, we should have lost this city forever, and the castles which belong to it.'

The knight and the ladies led Lancelot to the palace, where he was disarmed. From many places in the forest which surrounded the city, he heard the greatest joy in the world.

'Sir,' said the ladies, 'now you can hear the joy at your coming. It is the people and the inhabitants of the city who already know the news.'

Lancelot leaned out of the window of the hall, and saw the finest people in the world populating the city, and filling the great halls, and clerks and priests and great processions, praising and adoring God, because they could now return to their churches, and they gave thanks to the knight through whom they had the power to return. Lancelot was greatly honoured throughout the city. The two ladies took great pains to do him service.

From *Perlesvaus. Le Haut Livre Du Graal P*, ed. W.A. Nitze and T.A. Jenkins, Chicago 1932–7, pp. 136–8, 283–6.

The Girl with the Mule, or The Mule without a Bridle

The common man says in a proverb that what is most valuable is what is old and found in the past. And so by natural inclination and choice everyone must consider his own as most dear, for value is very soon attached to a thing which proves useful. Nowadays the old ways are less highly valued than the new ones, because the new are considered more attractive – and so they appear to be better; but often enough it happens that the old are more congenial. That is why Pagan of Maisières said that one should nevertheless cling to the old ways more than to the new.

Here begins an adventure about the girl with the mule who came to the court of King Arthur.

Once, on the day of Pentecost, it happened that King Arthur held court at Carlisle, as he always did, and so there were many knights gathered together from every land who had come to the court. With the queen there were both ladies and young girls (there were many beautiful ones) who had come to the court. They talked until the nobles, after eating, went away to amuse themselves in the hall above the upper rooms, and they looked down from the windows, across to a meadow. They had only been there a short time when they saw a solitary girl who was very graceful and beautiful, coming towards the castle at a great pace on a mule. So the lady came up, but she had no bridle on her mule – there was only a halter. The knights, with much talking and discussion among themselves, greatly marvelled what it could mean, and they said that the queen would certainly know, if she should stop there, for what pressing business she came to the land.

'Kay,' said Gawain, 'go and find her, and tell the king that he should come, that nothing should hinder him from coming to us immediately.'

The seneschal went off straight away to where both the queen and the king were.

'Sir,' said Kay, 'your knights beg you to come up here.'

And they at once asked him,

'Seneschal, what do they want of us?'

'Come with me,' he said, 'and I will explain to you; I will show you the strange thing that we have all seen.'

Meanwhile the girl came up and dismounted before the hall. Gawain went running to meet her, and many of the others ran too, and many helped and honoured her. But it plainly appeared from her manner that she did not have much wish to trifle, because she had had great trouble. The king sent for her and she was brought before him. As soon as she had come before the king, she greeted him:

'Sir,' she said, 'you can clearly see that I am very angry and sad. And every day it will be the same; I shall never be happy for a single day until my bridle is restored to me. It has been wrongfully taken from me, and because of this I have lost all my joy. I am sure that I shall regain it if there is a knight here who dares to take this upon him, and who is prepared to undertake this journey. And if he is willing to return it to me, I will be entirely his, as soon as I get my bridle back, without challenge and without opposition. And immediately and without delay I will do much for the love of him, for I will give him my mule to take him to a castle which is very well situated and strong and beautiful. But he will never be able to get it in peace.'

At these words Kay stepped forward, and he said that he would go to find the bridle, should it be in never so strange a land. But he wanted her to kiss him first, before he went away, and he wanted to kiss her straight away.

'Ha, sir,' she said, 'until you have the bridle, I do not intend to grant you the kiss. But when the bridle is restored, then the castle shall be given to you, and the kisses and the other thing.'

Kay did not dare to importune her further, and she repeated and impressed upon him that the mule should not be hindered from going as it wished to go. Kay did not care to remain there with them any longer. He went his way to the mule and mounted by the stirrup. He had no desire for an escort. When they saw that he had gone off all alone, with no companion, and carrying no weapon except only his sword, the girl kept on weeping because she could clearly foresee and was convinced that she would not have her bridle back.

So all that day he rode along on the mule, which went at a steady trot; and because it had well learnt the way, it carried him well. At last Kay had gone so far that there he was, deep in a forest, a forest tall and vast. But he had scarcely entered it than the beasts which lived in it all gathered round, lions and tigers and leopards. They all came up from every side because of Kay, who had to go through it, but before he could pass, a great many beasts who had come to meet him hastened up. Kay was afraid of them with a fear so great that there never was a greater. He said that he had only taken that way for the sole reason that he knew no other, or he would never have entered the wood. But the beasts, because of their knowledge of the lady, out of respect for the mule when they saw it, bent their knees to the ground; so in honour of the lady they knelt right down. And because those who lived in or came into the forest knew they were safe, they could not honour her more. But Kay had no wish to remain there; as soon as he could he went on his way. And every lion and leopard went away to his own lair.

Then Kay came to a little path, not very well-trodden, along which the mule made its way. The mule knew the path well, for it had been there many times and it led him out of the forest where he had suffered much distress. And here he is, out of the forest! But he had no sooner gone forward than he came to a valley which was very deep and wide and extremely perilous, very overshadowed and very dark. In the whole world there is no man so brave that he would not fear death if he had to pass through the valley. He had to pass through it immediately; willingly or not, he must enter it. He went in, because he could not do otherwise. He entered it with some trouble, and then to his astonishment he saw at the bottom of it, enormous snakes and serpents, scorpions and other creatures, who threw out fire from their heads, and at this he was very much afraid; and worse still, they gave off such a stink that, right from the hour when he was born, he never smelt such a smell. But he kept going so well that he did not fall, until he was a little way off from the smell. He said that he would rather be where he had been before, with the lions in the wood. There will never be a summer so hot, nor such burning heat, that there will not always be cold, as in the worst depths of winter, in that valley. I think that all the hatefulness of winter is always to be found there. There is always a north wind which the great cold traps there, and the other winds which blow continually battle together inside. There are so many harmful things that I could not tell half of them.

Kay nevertheless made so much effort that he came to the way out. Then he saw a plain, so he was a little reassured. Thus he went on so that he escaped from the fire and from the smell. He never thought to see the day when he would be out of that place.

He dismounted on the level ground and took off the saddle of the mule. Then he saw water in the middle of the meadow very close to a spring which was both very clear and very pure and which was very welcome there. It was entirely surrounded with flowers, with hawthorn and juniper. He watered his mule there now, because it had great need. He also drank from the spring to cool himself, as it seemed so beautiful. Then he turned his mule and put it once more to a trot because it seemed to him that the way was long. He never thought that he would find what he had set out to seek.

Kay went riding a long way until he came to a great stretch of water, but he was much dismayed when he saw that it was deep and wide and that there was neither ship nor barge nor any bridge or crossing. He went a long way along the bank until by chance he found a plank which was by no means wide. All the same, it might take him if he dared go on it, because it was all of iron. The crossing somewhat frightened him, since it looked very black to him, and he thought that he would be able to find no way to cross over. It would be better to return because he might come to grief here; he would be better advised to, and he said that he would be cursed if he would put himself in such peril for such a nonsense, for such a worthless matter. The way that he had come seemed to be too dangerous, but the crossing appeared to be even more perilous.

Then Kay turned round and so started on his way back. He kept carefully to the right path and so when he had reached the valley he went straight on to where he had found the stinking reptiles. He never stopped riding straight on through it until he got beyond it, and so he was in great bodily distress, broken down with weariness and exhausted. When he entered the forest where the wild beasts were, they came to meet him as soon as they saw him. They came running furiously towards him as if – I imagine – they would have eaten him, but they desisted on account of the mule to whom they owed honour. And Kay was so much afraid that for ten cities he would not have wanted to go into the wood, not even if by doing so he could have owned the whole of Pavia. Out of the wood, into the meadow he came, in front of the castle. King Arthur, who was very handsome, saw him returning and came to the window, and Gawain and Gahereth and Sir Yvain and Girflez and many other knights that he had called to him.

When they saw that the seneschal had come, they sent to search for the girl.

'Madam,' they said, 'come! You will have your bridle immediately for Kay has already arrived, and you may be sure that he has the bridle.'

But they lied, because he did not have it, and she called out in a loud voice:

'If he really did have it, he would never have returned so soon.'

Then she pulled at her hair and tore it. Who could bear to look upon the great suffering that she endured, and the grief!

'I shall die of my own free will,' she said to herself, 'if God will help me.'

But Gawain cheerfully said to her:

'Lady, grant me a request.'

'What, sir?'

'That you will not weep, but eat and so be happy. I shall be extremely miserable if I do not restore your bridle to you, and I will help you with all my heart.'

'Sir,' said she, 'do you tell me that I shall have my bridle for certain?'

'Yes, indeed.'

'Then I shall eat and be completely happy only if you promise it to me.'

Then Gawain took it upon him that if he should never achieve anything else, he would get it back again wherever it might be. Then the girl went out and came to the threshold of the hall, to her mule. Kay meanwhile had gone to his lodging very sad, extremely sorry and very distressed. The king thought it was no joke when the shameful deed that Kay had committed was told and recounted to him, and how because of it he did not dare to come to court. At that time Kay did not want to go on talking about it any longer, nor ever to hear of the lady and how she had come to the king.

The lady spoke to this effect: that Gawain had promised her that he would bring back the bridle, however strong a place it might be in, provided that he had leave to go.

'I agree to it very gladly,' said the king and the queen, who granted this request. And so Gawain made great haste, but first of all, before he went away, he wished to embrace her. It was appropriate that he should kiss her, and she kissed him very willingly. And now the girl was much at ease because she well knew, without any doubt, that she would have the bridle since it was Gawain who was going. So there was no need to plead. Gawain came to the mule and jumped into the saddle. The lady prayed for more than thirty blessings for him, and they all commended him to God. Gawain stopped there no longer but at once turned away from the place. But he had not left his sword behind.

He came to the meadow which took him on to the forest where the lairs of the wild beasts were, and the lion and the leopard now came over to the side where Gawain had to go. They went direct to meet him, and as soon as they saw the mule that they recognised again, they bent their knees to the ground and humbled themselves towards the knight in love and recognition. And that was the sign that he would bring back the bridle by force, be it in never so strong a place. But when Gawain saw the creatures he was convinced beyond a doubt that Kay was afraid when he passed through, and returned because of that. Laughing at it, he went on to where a little path came in which led him straight to the valley which was so polluted. So he went on without stopping, not fearing anything. Eventually he came to another part, down into the middle of the plain where the beautiful spring was. He took the saddle off the mule and rubbed it down and resaddled it again. He hardly lingered there, because the journey was so difficult. Gawain kept on going and so came to the black water which was more turbulent than the Loire. I do not want to say any more about it – never was anything so ugly seen, nor so horrible, nor so cruel, nor do I know how to describe it to you, and so I can only say, without invention, that it is the river of the devil in both appearance and actuality, nor does one see anything but devils there. And there was no place to cross. So he went along the bank until he found the plank which was no more than an inch or two wide, but all of iron. He was a little anxious about crossing, both because he was sure that Kay, before him, did not dare to go, and because he had turned back from the place.

Gawain commended himself to God. He struck the mule and it sprang onto the plank, which did not give way, but it often happened that part of its hoof was over the plank. It is not surprising if he was afraid, although it was the bending of the plank that caused him the greatest fear. He got across with some difficulty, but this thing is certain, that if the mule had not known the way, it would have fallen. On this occasion it kept itself from falling. Then he went on his way, as fortune decreed and destined. He went along a little path which took him towards a castle which was very well situated, strong and beautiful.

The castle was so very strong that it need fear no attack. It was enclosed all the way round with a great moat, both broad and deep, and in the same way it was entirely surrounded with great stakes, very pointed and big, and on each one of the stakes, except for one, where it was lacking, there was the head of a knight. Gawain had no intention of giving up. The castle did not have a door or a gate – it was turning very rapidly, like a windmill that revolves, or like the top that you spin with a cord. Gawain was ready to enter it at once, although he marvelled very greatly at it and asked himself what it meant and what it could be. He greatly desired to know what it was, but he was not afraid. Then on the drawbridge, he stopped before the gate and his boldness forced him to act bravely, not to turn back. The castle kept on turning, but he said that however it might be, cost what it might, he would get in. It was very awkward for him, because as soon as the door was before him, it immediately went past him. He considered his position very carefully, and said that he would go in when the door through which he had to enter was in front of him. Then he saw the door come round so he spurred the mule furiously and it jumped because of the spur and broke in the door, but it was caught from behind so that almost half its tail was cut off. So he got through the door. And the mule, who rejoiced to see it, took him right into the lanes of the castle; but he was a little anxious when he saw inside it neither man, woman nor child. He came right up under the porch of a house, and as soon as he had dismounted, a dwarf came down the street in a great hurry and as he greeted him, so he replied:

'You are welcome.'

Gawain, too, was not slow but immediately returned his greeting and said to him:

'Dwarf, who are you? Who is your lady, and who is your lord?'

But the dwarf would not say any more, and immediately went away. Gawain could not understand what he had seen and wondered to himself why it was the dwarf would not answer. Should he deign to capture him? Then it might suit him to give a reason! However, he allowed him to go free; now he sprang to the ground. He saw, under an archway, a vast cellar which went very deep underground. He said that he wanted to explore all the inner passages before he went on; he would not think very highly of himself if he did not discover what it all was. Then, lo and behold, he saw, coming slowly up from the cellar, a very hairy churl. It could well be said that Gawain had seen something which made his journey useless. The churl looked very evil, and he was bigger than St. Marcel. On his shoulder he carried a huge, broad axe. Gawain was much astonished when he saw the churl, who looked like a Moor of Mauretania, or one of those louts from Champagne who are completely tanned by the sun. He stopped in front of Gawain and then greeted him. And Gawain took a good look at his face and his figure.

'May you have good luck!' he said.

'Well may you say that!' said Gawain.

'Yes, indeed, I consider you a brave man to have come in here. Your journey has been a waste of time, for the bridle that you have come here to seek could not be in a safer place. It has very good guards around it. It will be essential for you to put up a great fight, so help me God, before you possess it.'

'You do not frighten me in the least,' said Gawain. 'I shall certainly give you fighting enough, so help me God; I shall die rather than give up the bridle.'

And he delayed no longer, but because he saw that it was getting dark, the churl set about accommodating him and led him straight to a lodging and took the trouble to make him sit down. The mule was well stabled. The churl took a large white towel and two bowls and gave them to Gawain to wash his hands, for there were no other servants there. The table was already laid, and Gawain sat down to eat, for he was very hungry. And the churl gave him a great quantity and served him to his pleasure. As soon as he had eaten, the churl removed the table and brought him the water. He provided a huge bed, both high and broad, for Gawain so that he could lie down, because he longed to rest, as befits such a knight. Now the churl came towards him again.

'Gawain,' he said, 'you shall lie alone all night long in this bed, without challenge and without opposition. But, in peace, I ask you this, before you lie down, because I have heard you praised. I now propose to you a test, and because I know my right, undertake it freely.'

And Gawain promised him that he would accept it whatever it was.

'Tell me now,' said Gawain, 'what is it? So help me God, I will take it on. I will not deceive you by any word spoken to my good host.'

'Cut off my head tonight,' he said, 'with this sharp axe; and as you behead me, by the same reckoning I shall cut off your head in the morning, when I come back. Now get on with it without arguing,' he said.

'I should be very ignorant,' said Gawain, 'if I did not know what I am undertaking. I will take whatever comes: tonight I will cut off yours, and in the morning I shall offer you mine, if you wish me to do so.'

'May evil befall anyone who asks for better,' said the churl. 'Now come on then!'

Then he showed him the way. The churl placed his neck on a block, then Gawain took the axe, and he cut off the head with one blow – he lost no time in doing it. The churl jumped up at once on his feet, and took his head; he returned to the cellar and Gawain went back and lay down to sleep straight away. He slept soundly until morning.

Next day, as soon as it was light, Gawain got up and prepared himself. Then, believe it or not, the churl came back quite safe and sound, with his axe on his shoulder. Now Gawain might well consider himself a fool when he saw the head that he had cut off. But he did not fear him at all, and the churl who was not in the least the worse for it, spoke.

'Gawain,' he said, 'I have come to remind you of the agreement.'

'I do not dispute it in the least, for I clearly see that it must be done; one cannot fight against it.'

And so he had to act bravely, for he did not wish to be disloyal, because of the agreement that he had made. He said that he would willingly keep to it.

'Come here then,' said the churl.

Out came Gawain from inside. He held out his neck on the block and the churl said to him straightaway:

'Uncover your neck completely.'

'I have no more, by God!' he said, 'but strike if you want to strike.'

It would have been a very great pity and tragedy if he had struck him, so help me God! He lifted his axe right up – which he did to frighten him – but he did not intend to touch him because he was so loyal and because he had so well kept his promise to him. And Gawain asked him how he could get the bridle.

'You shall certainly know,' he said. 'As soon as noon is past you will have fighting enough, so that you will not feel inclined to boast, because you will have to fight with two lions now chained up. The bridle is not quite unprotected; rather, it has a terrible guard; or may fearful fire and fierce flame burn me! If there were ten knights, I know very well that no-one who undertook to fight them could ever escape the two fierce lions without my help! So you must eat a little since you are going to the fight, for your heart must not fail you, but you must be stronger.'

'To eat will not help in any way,' said Gawain, 'but find me some good armour in which I can equip myself.'

'In here,' said the churl, 'there is a good horse which no-one has ridden for months, and there is enough armour as well, which I shall gladly provide you with. But first I shall show you the animals, so that you will be prepared, and so as to discover if you would rather give up the fight with the lions.'

'So help me, St Pantelions,' said Gawain, 'I will not see them until I am ready to fight them; but arm me immediately.'

And the churl armed him at once with good armour from head to foot, for he well knew how to do it properly; and then he brought him the warhorse. Gawain mounted by the stirrup, not in the least afraid. The churl brought him seven shields which would be very useful to him, and then he went to release one of the lions and led it in, and the lion was raging with such great fury and great fierceness that it tore up the ground with its claws and gnawed its chain with its teeth. When it was right outside and it saw the knight it began to bristle and to lash its tail. Indeed anyone who fought with it needed to know the art of sword-play. It would not do for him to have the heart of a goat or a slug. The churl let it go in a flat place in front of him and Gawain did not deign to draw back, so he attacked with his drawn sword, and he struck at the lion's lifted head and the lion struck him again. There was a good interchange of blows between the two. At the first blow the lion struck him so that it dashed away the shield and tore it from him. The churl armed him with another, and Gawain took it. He struck the lion savagely on its back with his sword, but the hide was hard and dry, so hard that he could not pierce it. The lion was merely angry and so came back again with fury and struck Gawain again on the head with its paw, and tore away the second and the third shield, so that he had need of a fourth.

'Now by my beard you are too slow,' said the churl.

Then Sir Gawain struck the lion surely and pierced it right to its entrails with the full length of his sword, so that the beast was dead.

'Now let the other come to me,' he said, and the churl released it. It showed great distress and was much angered on account of its companion, whom it saw lying dead. It came straight towards the knight and then attacked with such strength that it struck away the shield at the first blow. Then the churl supplied another and advised Gawain as best he could. The lion came at him running and attacked him fiercely from the front; its claws tore all his chainmail up to his ventail, and so it again wrenched his shield from him, and the churl gave him another. But now Gawain saw and clearly realised that if the lion tore that one away, it would be a very serious matter. He struck the lion along the parting on its head with his sharp sword, so that he cleft it in two right to the teeth, and the lion fell to the ground.

'That is the end of the battle,' said Gawain, 'and peace is made. Now give me the bridle immediately, for the faith that you owe your father.'

'By Saint Peter, it is not,' said the churl. 'There is no need of a trick. Already I see that all the sleeve of your hauberk is red with blood. If you wish to take my advice, you will disarm yourself and take some food so as to strengthen yourself.'

But no pain could make him willing to do so, and the churl took him right in through the rooms and through the doors, for he well knew all the inner passages, until he came straight into the room where lay the knight who was wounded in the body.

'You are welcome, Gawain,' he said as soon as he saw him. 'Fortune has sent you here, for now I am healed already; and as you are strong enough you must now do battle with me.'

Since it could not be otherwise, Gawain said that he would not oppose it. And now the knight got up and immediately armed himself to his satisfaction. But I almost omitted something which I ought not to omit, so I must explain how it was that the wounded man got up. He had a certain custom, that when a knight from another land came on behalf of the girl to seek for the bridle which was there, he had to fight him. And if he was vanquished by him, the prize for victory would not be given, except to have his head cut off and then fixed on one of the stakes with which the castle was surrounded. And if it turned out adversely for him, so that he was overcome by him, another stake would be set up so that another knight could come whom he would vanquish in battle.

So they were both armed, and the churl brought each of them a good warhorse, and they mounted without stirrups. And the shields hung from their necks; soon the blows would be heard. When they were mounted the churl brought two great lances to give them, so that they could begin the battle. Then they moved away from each other and came together without resting their lances. They gave each other such blows, in their great strength, that they were almost unhorsed. The lances broke and splintered and the saddle broke behind and the stirrups broke; only the girth was left to break, which could not bear the weight. They had to come down to the ground and encounter each other on foot at once, holding their shields on their arms. Fiercely they strove to strike: they dealt such blows on the shields that the sparks flew from them. With their swords they struck the shields so that the pieces fell away. For two long stretches they fought together, but only one foot of land could one gain from the other. Gawain exhausted the knight so much that he fell back, so he attacked him with great strength, and soon cut his helmet in two and cut through the circlet. And so he was stunned and struck down to the ground, and Gawain clutched him firmly, seizing him with great anger and acting as if he was going to kill him, and he immediately cried out:

'Gawain, do not kill me. I was foolish when I took you on, but even this morning I thought that there was no knight under heaven who dared encounter me; but you have overcome me by force, so now this shows that you are of great worth. And I thought that I would cut off your head and fix it on this stake, on which there is no head fixed, just as I have cut off those all around the palace from knights who have come here for just such an affair. So I thought I would serve you, but under heaven there is no such knight as you.'

Gawain let him go, and he went off; Gawain was disarmed in his room.

'Churl,' said Gawain, 'now think how I am to get the bridle.'

'Gawain,' said he, 'do you want to know what you have to do first? You have got to fight with two dragons, menacing and

fierce, who squirt blood in every direction and breathe fire from
their mouths. But you may be sure that this armour will not avail
you in this need. I am going to bring you another which is
stronger and more durable. There are at least four hundred
hauberks of mail both strong and undamaged in here, which
belonged to those knights whose severed heads you see.'

The churl quickly brought in armour of all kinds. He gave
Gawain a suit of armour both strong and intact, so as to equip
him well. Then Gawain said:

'Go and bring the infernal creatures you mentioned.'

[A line of the original is missing here.]

The churl said:

'When it is past mid-day you will have enough to do. Apart
from me, there is not a man under heaven so brave that he dare
approach them, or even dare look at them.'

Gawain replied:

'Do not worry.'

Then the churl went to loose the dragons, which were both very
fierce and big, and he brought them right in. Very savage
creatures they were, and whichever way Gawain turned, from
one side to the other, his shield was caught by their fire. He
attacked them with all his might; such a blow he struck with his
sword (so the writings attest) that he cut off the head of one, and
so killed it instantly. I do not know how to set about describing it.
But when midday was past, he had so disposed of both of them,
that both were dead and decapitated. He was somewhat smeared
about his face with blood and with filth. The churl took back from
Gawain the suit of armour in which he fought.

As soon as he was disarmed, the little dwarf came to him (the
one who had come to him first under the porch and greeted him
but who did not condescend to speak further, and had gone away
very proudly).

'Gawain,' he said, 'on behalf of my lady, I offer you service, on
condition that you will eat with her; and at your will you shall
acquire, entirely without hindrance and without fighting, the
bridle that you have come to seek.'

Then Gawain said that he would go if the churl would conduct
him, for he had great reliance in him. Hand in hand they went
together, and very well the churl led him. They went through
room after room until they came straight to the room where the

lady who had sent the dwarf to search for Sir Gawain was lying in a bed. Now that he had come, she saw him. He went up to her and she said to him:

'Gawain, you are very welcome. But it is a great grief and sorrow to me that all my wild beasts are now dead in this way because of your coming. All the same, you should eat with me now. Never, indeed, have I known a better or a more valiant knight than you.'

They sat together on the bed, but it was not, I believe, a bed either of willow or of poplar on which the lady and Gawain sat, for the four posts of the bed were all of fine silver gilded and on top there was brocade embroidered with little circles and all worked with stones, and plenty of other rich adornments. If I wanted to describe them to you, I should very soon use up my time, but there is no need to speak of them. Water for washing was called for, and the churl now brought the golden bowls, and he brought the towel, too, for them to dry on. Then they sat down to eat, the lady and Sir Gawain. The dwarf and the churl served them, for there were no other servants there. The lady was very much at her ease and made good cheer with her guest. She very soon made him sit by her, side by side, and eat from one dish with her. Greatly she praised him, greatly she prized him. Meanwhile I shall make mention of nothing else; no more shall I tell you now. But when they had eaten and the table had been carried away, water was asked for by the lady and the churl immediately offered it to her. Gawain was delayed from going, for she much desired to delay him. Then he asked the lady for the bridle which he well deserved to have.

'Sir,' she said, 'I put my power and myself at your service in this way because you have undertaken a very great thing for my sister. I am her sister and she is mine, so I ought to honour you highly. If it pleases you to remain here, I will take you for my lord and give up the whole of this castle to you, and the thirty-eight others I have besides.'

'Madam,' he said, 'don't trouble yourself. I am already late, I tell you on my honour, in returning to the court of the king, to whom I have made a promise. But give me the bridle that I have come to seek at once. I have already been too long in this land as it is, and I will not stay longer. Nevertheless I am greatly obliged to you for the boon that you offer me.'

'Gawain,' she said, 'take the bridle – see it there on that silver nail.'

He immediately took it, and great was the joy that he expressed. Then the churl brought in the mule, Gawain put on the bridle and the saddle, and took his leave of the lady. She ordered the churl that he should enable Sir Gawain to go without hindrance and that he should make the castle stand quite still until he had gone away. Sir Gawain mounted, very glad to be on his way. The churl ordered that the castle should be quite still, and so it was. Gawain safely departed and when he had passed the bridge, he looked back at the castle. Then he saw in all the streets great companies of people dancing caroles and displaying such great joy, that if God had commanded it, there could not have been more rejoicing. They amused themselves with one another. The churl who had led him outside was still at the door, and Gawain asked him what the meaning of it was, for he had seen no-one, great or small, go into the castle, and now he saw joy so great that people were actually dancing for joy inside.

'Sir,' said the churl, 'they had all taken refuge in those cellars, because of the savagery of the beasts that you have killed. They made such a very great noise that if ever the people happened to come out for any reason, there was nothing for it but to unleash them, whatever the consequences. And because of their fierceness and fury they rushed out to tear the people in pieces. And now they are saying in their own language that through you God has delivered them, and has illuminated with many blessings the people who were in darkness. Such is the great joy they feel at what they see – such joy that it could not be greater.'

You may be quite certain, in truth, that this was very pleasing to Gawain. Now he set out on the path which led him straight towards the water, where the iron plank was. He went across in safety. He went riding so far after that, that he reached the valley which was filled with reptiles and passed out in safety. He came into the forest where the wild beasts were and as soon as they saw him they went right up to him and accompanied him, bent their knees to the ground and were happy to approach him. They kissed his feet and his legs, and did the same to the mule. Gawain came out of the forest; he was not slow in his going, and came on to the plain which was close to the castle. King Arthur and the Queen had gone to amuse themselves, and with them many knights who were of their company, from the hall and the upper rooms. And Gawain came on without stopping. The queen saw him first and pointed him out to the knights. They went to meet him – both the knights and the ladies. The lady was very happy at the news when she heard that Sir Gawain, who must have the bridle, had come. Sir Gawain had come, and the girl went to meet him.

'Sir,' she said, 'may God give you a good meeting, and all the pleasure that anyone could have, both day and night.'

'And good fortune to you, too,' said he, dismounting from the mule by his silver stirrup. The girl took him in her arms and kissed him more than a hundred times.

'Sir,' she said, 'it is quite right that I should freely place my body itself at your service, for I can assure you that I have not received the bridle from any man that I have managed to send to the castle. For in consequence many knights are dead, who had their heads cut off and so had no power to take it.'

Then Gawain told her of the adventures that he had experienced: of the great valley and of the wood, and of the fountain by the bushes, and of the black water, and of the castle that revolved, and of the lions that he killed and of the knight that he overcame, and of the churl's compact, and of the battle with the dragons, and of the dwarf who greeted him and did not condescend to say more, and how afterwards he returned, and how he had to eat in the room of the lady who was sister to the girl, and how the bridle was given up, and when he got out of the castle, how he had seen the caroles in the streets, and how he came out without hindrance and without trouble.

When Gawain had related all this, and the girl had taken leave of the nobles of the court, Queen Guinevere came running and the king and the knights went to beg her to stay there with them, and to give her love to one of the knights of the Round Table.

'Sir,' she said, 'God condemn me if I should hesitate to stay if I were free; but I cannot remain, come what may.'

She asked for her mule, and someone brought it. She mounted by the stirrup and the king went to set her on her way, but she said that she wished to have no escort, lest it should be a trouble to them, as it was rather late. She took her leave and so went away, putting her mule into a trot. This is the end of the adventure of the lady with the mule who went off all on her own.

La Damoiselle à la Mule (La Mule Sanz Frain) by Paien de Maisières, ed. B. Orlowski, Paris 1911.

(See also *Two Old French Gauvain Romances* ed. R.C. Johnston and D.D.R. Owen, Scottish Academic Press, 1972. Texts of *Le Chevalier à l'Epée* and *La Mule Sans Frein* with Introduction, Notes and Glossary, and Parallel Readings with *Sir Gawain and the Green Knight*.)

From Hunbaut

Gawain, travelling with another knight, called Hunbaut, is challenged
to a beheading game which has a surprising outcome.

There was no castle better constructed in the world, nor a more
magnificent, nor a better situated one, and they found a churl
sitting there on the left, in front of the gate, and a boy brought
him an axe in his two hands.

'Hunbaut,' he said, 'if anybody attacks me, I will have my
rights with this.'

He stood upright on his feet so that nothing could be seen
beyond him. He certainly seemed an evil-natured man; he was
big and black, ugly and hideous. He looked at both the knights
and barred the way to them. Hunbaut asked him, nevertheless, to
wait until they returned. He gave no sign of having understood.
He held his axe in both hands. And Gawain said:

'Now we shall have something to do here before we leave. I do
not know what right he demands.'

And Hunbaut said:

'One choice is open to you which I can explain to you very well,
but it is very dangerous to take it. There is trouble both on the one
hand and on the other. You can cut off his head with that axe at
once but it will not guarantee your safety. He proffers and gives
his neck up to you on the understanding that you offer your neck
to him immediately afterwards. And he will keep close to you and
will hold the axe in his hand. He will offer no more nor less to you
than a single blow – no more. The choice is offered: there is no
other. Take whichever will please you. Do not act wrongly in any
way towards the churl who offers the choice.'

And Gawain replied:

'I will never go elsewhere for advice; I will advise myself. I
grant you whatever it is he wants. Give me that axe first. I shall
not make a mistake when I have placed my life in jeopardy.'

[Some lines appear to be missing here.]

Gawain said:

'I will do it first because I do not want to strike in the way that
the other two agreed, and that I have already noted.'

Then the churl held out the axe to him, and then he extended
his neck before him without hesitation, and certainly thought that

he would be safe, nor did he think of having any protection. Sir Gawain looked at him – he had seen many a marvel, so that he was not greatly astonished, but felt greatly encouraged; for he felt himself big and strong, and he held a sharp axe. He thought carefully about the stroke, and of the great blow that he was forced to strike – Gawain who summoned all his strength there. Indeed, I can assure you that he did not make a feint; instead, he made the wretch's head fly far away, more than ten paces. And the churl opened both his fists, for he intended to go after it immediately. Sir Gawain, who was aware of the enchantment, kept near. He seized the churl by the clothes, because that was necessary for his purpose, and the magic failed, for the churl fell dead on the spot and the magic was brought to an end, so that the double game was never again offered there.

Then Sir Gawain and Hunbaut left that place, joyous and relieved that they had thus passed through the adventure.

From *Hunbaut* ed. J. Sturzinger and H. Breuer, Dresden 1914, lines 1462–1539.

THREE

The Passing of the Year

From Kyng Alisaunder

The author of *Kyng Alisaunder* speaks of the diversity of human experience:

> Divers is this myddell erde
> To lewede men and to lerede.
> Bysynesse, care and sorowe
> Is with man vche morowe
> Som for seknesse and somme for smerte
> Som for defaute other poverte
> Som for the lyves drede
> That glyt away as flour in mede.
> Ne is lyves man non so slyghe
> That he ne tholeth ofte ennoye
> In mony cas, in mony manere,
> Whiles he lyveth in werlde here.   (1–12)

(Adverse is this world both to ignorant and to learned men. Toil, care and sorrow is man's lot every day. Some is because of sickness and some because of pain, some because of want or poverty, some because of fear for their lives that fade away like the flowers of the field. Nor is there a living man so wise that he does not often suffer distress in many situations, in many ways while he lives here in this world.)

The month of April:

> Averylle is mery and longith the daye
> Levedyes dauncen and thai playe.
> Swaynes justeth, knyghtis tournay,
> Syngeth the nightyngale, gradeth the jay;

61

The hote sunne clyngeth the clay,
As ye wel yseen may.   (139–44)

(April is merry and the days get longer. Ladies dance and amuse
themselves, young men joust, knights engage in tournaments, the
nightingale sings, the jay chatters. The hot sun hardens the clay, as
you can clearly see.)

The month of May:

In tyme of Maij the nighttyngale
In wood maketh mery gale.
So don the foules, grete and smale,
Summe on hylles and summe in dale.   (2543–46)

(In the month of May the nightingale sings a merry song in the wood.
So do the birds, both great and small, some on the hills and some in
the dales.)

Autumn:

Whan corne ripeth in heruest-tyde,
Mery it is in felde and hyde.
Synne it is and shame to chide,
For shameful dedes springeth wyde.
Knighttes willeth on huntyng ride –
The dere galpeth by wode-syde.   (457–62)

(When the corn ripens at harvest time it is delightful in the fields and
meadows. It is sinful and shameful to complain, for shameful deeds
spring up all around. Knights wish to go hunting; the deer pants at
the edge of the wood.)

Harvest-time returns again:

In tyme of hervest mery it is ynough –
Peres and apples hongeth on bough,
The hayward bloweth mery his horne,
In everyche felde ripe is corne,
The grapes hongen on the vyne.
Swete is trewe love and fine!   (5745–50)

(At harvest time it is most delightful. Pears and apples hang on the
bough, the herdsman merrily blows his horn. In every field the corn
is ripe, the grapes hang on the vine. Sweet is true and noble love.)

From *Kyng Alisaunder* ed. G.V. Smithers, Early English Text Society,
London 1952, vol. I.

From the Secretum Secretorum

Of the .iiij. seasons of the yere

OVre intencion is to declare in this book the .iiij. ceasons of the yere, and the qualite and propirte of yche of thaim, and the contrariete and difference of the same. Whiche ceasons ben diuided as here-aftir folowith, that is to sey: vere, somyr, autumpne, and wynter. Veer begynneth whan the sun entrith in the signe of Aries and endureth .iiij.xxxiij dayes, x[x]iij. houres, and the fourth parte of an houre, that is to wite, from the xth. day of the ende of Marche unto the xxiijti day of June. And in this ceason ben the nyghtys and the dayes egall in thaire regions. The tyme is swete, the wyndes risen, the snowes meltyn, the ryvers enforcen thaire cours, and the humors of the erthe taken heete, whiche ascendith to the height of trees, and causeth thaim to flourish. The medues refresshen thaire verdure, all maner seede and corne springeth and groweth, alle maner floures taken thaire fressh colours. And the birdes renwen thaire fressh clothinge, and payn thaim to vtter thaire swete and melodious songes. The trees ben spredde with greene leuys and floures, beestes engendren, and alle thinges taken might and vertu. The erthe taketh beaute, which is like to the faire spouse that is clothid in riche and precious clothinge, which causeth to seeme miche fairere.

Of the ceason of veer and what it is

WEer is hote, and temperate with humor. In this ceason mannys bloode meeuith and spreedith in all the membres of the bodye, and the body takith perfite compleccion. And in this ceson shuld be eiten chikenys, kyddes, and egges till .vi. and no moo at onys, and eite letuse that is egre, whiche is called in som cuntree karioles. Eite also gotes mylke. And in this ceason is bettir to be lat bloode than in any othir ceason. And allso it is good to trauayle, and to haue the bely softe, and to swete, and walke, and to bath him-self, and to eite suche meites as will purge well the baily, for all the wastinge that thou shall haue through bleedinge or digestion is soon recouerde.

The ceason of somyr and what it is

SOmyr begynneth whan the sun entreth in the first pointe of the signe of the Crabbe, and endureth iiijxxxij daies, xxiijti houres, and the iijd parte of an houre, that is to say, from the xxiijti day of June vnto the xxiiijti day of Septembre. In this ceason ben longe dayes and shorte nyghtys. And in all regions the hete encrecith, and the wyndes swage, the see is pleasaunt and meeke, the aere is swete, the cornys drien, the serpentes growen and cast out thaire venyme. The vertu of mannys body is fortified and perfourmed, and alle the worlde is replenysht with goodys. And this ceason is likenyd to the spouse that is faire and plesaunt in hir parfite age. And this ceason is hoot and drye. And beware of all thinges that ben of hote and drye compleccion duringe this tyme.
(There follows more specific advice on the preservation of health during this season.)

Of the ceason of autumpne, and what he is

[A]Utumpne entreth whan the sonne entreth in the first degree of the Leon, and lasteth .iiijxx and viij. dayes, and .xxvij. houres, that is to sey, from the xxiiij. day of Septembre vnto the xxijti day of [Dec]embre. In this ceason, the nyghtes and the daies ben egall of lenght. The aire troubleth, the wyndres entren in thaire region, ryuers and springes discreecyn, the gardyn drieth, the frutes waxen ripe, the beaute of the erthe fadith, the birdes seekyn the warme cuntreis, the beestes axen the cauys and warme places, the serpentes seekyn thaire repaire, where they gete thaire liuinge for wynter. The erthe is as the olde womman that is naked, and passed youthe, and age draweth neere. The tyme is colde and drye. And therefore, this ceason, eite hoote meytes . . .
(Advice follows as before on the preservation of health.)

Of wynter ceason, and what it is

WYntyr begynneth whan the sun entreeth in the first degree of the signe of Aries, and endureth .lxx[x]ix. daies and xxiijti houres from the xxijti day of [Dec]embre vnto the xxti day of Marche. In this ceason, the daies ben shorte and the nyghtes ben longe, the colde is grete, the wyndes ben sharpe, the leuys fallyn downe, and alle thinges lose thaire verdoure for the moost parte. And the bestes rasoorten to cauys or dykes for the grete colde, the aire and the tyme waxeth blak, and the erthe is like to a womman of grete age, naked, and in decrepitude nygh to deth. And by-cause the wynter ys cold and moist, it is good to vse of hoote meytes . . .

From *The Secrete of Secretes* from University College, Oxford, MS. 85, in *Secretum Secretorum* Vol. I, ed. M.A. Manzalaoui, Early English Text Society, Oxford University Press, 1977, pp. 344–348.

The 'sesouns of ye yeer' from Lydgate's version
of the Secretum Secretorum

What tyme the sesoun / is Comyng of the yeer,
The hevenly bawme / Ascendyng from the Roote,
The ffresh Sesoun / of lusty grene veer,
Which quyketh Corages / and doth hertys boote,
When Rounde buddys / appere on braunchys soote,
The growyng tyme / and the yong sonne;
I mene the sesoun / whan veer is be gonne.

And bright phebus / Entryth the Rammys hed,
And begynneth / Ascendyn in his spere,
Whan the Crowne / of Alceste whyte and Red,
Aurora passyd / ful fresshly doth Appere;
ffor Ioye of which / with hevenly nootys clere,
The bryddys syngen /in ther Armonye.
Salwe that sesoun / with sugryd mellodye.

Twen hoot and moyst / this veer is temperat,
Havyng his moysture / of Wyntres sharp shours,
Of somyr folwyng / to fflora consecrat,
Hath moderat heete / be Recoord of Auctours;
The sesoun Ordeyned / taraye with newe Clours,
As gardeyns Erbys / and to sowe seedys,
And the lusty Silvir dewh / in the grene meedys.

Entrying this sesoun / wyntir doth leve take,
ffrostys departyd / and molte with the sonne,
And euery ffoul / Chosen hath his make,
And nytyngales / for Ioye her song hath be gonne;
Yonge Rabettys / be to ther Claperys Ronne,
And the Cokkow / that in Wyntir dare
In euery lay to synge / she lyst nat for to spare.

Lovers of Custom / do this sesoun preyse,
And yonge folkys / flouryng in tendir Age,
Erly a morwen / Tytan makith hem Aryse;
So Can nature / prykke them in ther Corage,
Walkynge by Ryvaylles / holdyng ther passage
On plesaunt hylles / so holsom is the Ayr,
Havyng great Ioye / the wedir is so ffayr.

When the new season is coming the heavenly balm rises up from the root – the fresh season of lusty green spring which raises the spirits and does the heart good – when round buds appear on the lovely branches – the time of growth and of the young sun – I mean the season when spring begins;

and bright Phoebus [the sun] enters the Ram's head and begins to ascend in his sphere, when the crown of Alcestis the white and red has passed Aurora and appears very brightly – for joy of this with clear, heavenly notes the birds sing in harmony. Greet that season with sweet melody.

Between heat and moistness the spring is temperate, taking its moisture from the sharp showers of winter; from the following summer, consecrated to Flora, it has moderate heat, as the authorities tell us. The season was ordained to bring forth new grass, as also the herbs in gardens, and for the sowing of seeds, and the fresh silvery dew in the green meadows.

When this season begins, winter takes his leave. The frosts have departed, melted with the sun, and every bird has chosen his mate, and nightingales have begun their song of joy. Young rabbits run to their burrows and the cuckoo that in winter lies low does not cease to sing continually.

Lovers customarily praise this season, as do young people flourishing in their youth – early in the morning Titan [the sun] makes them rise; nature so stirs up their hearts, walking by small streams and making their way over pleasant hills in great delight, for the air is so fresh and the weather is so fine.

Wherfore Alisaundir / whoo so take hede,
And lyst consydre / by good Avisement,
Of our yong Age / Accounte we must in dede
How that we hau / dyspendid our talent,
Outhir lyk foolys / or lyk folkys prudent,
To us commytted / whyl we haue been here,
To for the Iuge / whan we shal appere.

Next than folowith the sesoun Callid Estas

Now veer is past / with al his grene levys,
Aprylle and May / with hire sharp shours,
The silver dewh / in woodys and in grevys,
hath spred his bawme / On bankys & on clours;
And next folwyth Estas / with his somyr flours,
As seith thes clerkys / by discrypcioun,
Is hoot and drye / of Complexioun.

This tyme gynneth / soone vpon Barnabe:
Iune, Iule, August / lastith this sesoun,
Endith in Septembre / the sonne in Virgine
Hoot and drye / of disposicyoun,
And Coleryk / of Complexioun,
As is Remembryd / of Auctours Olde,
Endith with Bertylmew / with his dewys colde.

Ffyr, Colour, Estas / and Juventus Age,
To-gidre Accorde / in heete and drynesse,
And Coleryk men / Citryn of visage,
Rough, slyh, and Angry / Sume haue gret hardynesse
Off growing slaundre / fumous of hastynesse
With smoke and ffyr / haue greet Accordaunce,
ffuryous of Ire / froward of dalyaunce.

In this sesoun / Rypith frut and Corn,
A tyme ful notable / be Comendacyoun,
This tyme of yeer / Baptist Iohn was born,
Petir & Poule / suffryd passyoun,
And petrys cheynes / wer brooke in prysoun;
The feeste therof / Callyd lammesse,
And the translacyoun of Thomas / martryd in Crystemasse.

Therefore, Alexander, take heed of this and choose to consider thoughtfully, that we must indeed give an account of our youth, of how we have made use of our gifts — either like fools or like prudent folk — [which have been] committed to us while we have been here, when we shall appear before the Judge.

Next follows the season called Summer

Now spring is past with all its green leaves, April and May with their sharp showers. The silver dew in woods and groves has spread its balm on banks and on grassy ground. And next follows summer with its summer flowers, [which] as the clerks have described it, is hot and dry in its nature.

This time begins soon after St Barnabas's day [11th June]. Through June, July and August this season lasts. It ends in September when the sun is in Virgo, and its disposition is to be hot and dry. Its temperament is Choleric, as ancient authors remind us. It ends at St Bartholomew's tide [24 August], with its cold dews.

Fire, Choler, Summer and Youthfulness agree together in heat and dryness, and choleric men with their yellow faces [are] rough, sly and angry — some have great hardihood. Often breeding slander, furious and impatient, they have great affinity with smoke and fire, raging in anger, perverse in conversation.

In this season fruit and corn ripen. It is a memorable, most commendable time. St John the Baptist was born at this time of year [24 June], St Peter and St Paul were martyred [29 June], and St Peter's chains were broken in the prison [St Peter ad Vincula, 1 August]. The feast of this time is called Lammas [1 August], and it is the time of the translation [transference to a later day of a feast with which a feast of higher rank coincides] of St Thomas, martyred at Christmas.

Been at mydsoomyr / bryng hoony to ther hyvys,
The lyllyes whyte / Abrood ther levys sprede,
Beestys pasture / and shade hem vndir levys,
Ageyn the sonne / gras deyeth in the mede,
Chapelettys be maad / of Roosys whyte and Rede,
And euery thyng / drawith to his Rypyng,
As it faryth be man / in his Age growyng.

Strawberyes, Cheryes / in gardeynes men may se
Benys Rype / and pesecoddys grene,
Ageyn heetys / whan men distempryd be
ffolkys gadre purslane / and letuse that be Clene.
This sesoun fflora / that is of fflours quene,
Hire ffressh motlees / she tournyth now Citryne,
The vertu of herbys / doth doun ageyn declyne.

In this processe / it nedith not to tarye,
But Oonly to god / Set thyn Inward entent,
O Alisaundre / herte and thought nat varye,
But thank the lord / of what thing / that he sent,
Povert or Rychesse / ther-with to be content;
As god disposith / ther in to haue plesaunce,
As Oon in god / and god thy Suffysaunce.

ffor by the sentence / of Seyntes and of clerkys,
Of thy discertys / afftir the Rekenyng,
And lyk the ffrutys / of thy good werkys,
Thou shalt be guerdownyd / this soth and no lesyng,
With pees Eternal / last at thyn Endyng,
With Cryst to Regne / in the hevenly consistorye,
Whan thou by tryvmphe / hast of thy foon victorye.

Than folowith after the Thridde sesoun callid Autumpne

This tyme of Custom / set folkys in besynesse.
Ech tydy man / yevith him to travaylle,
To Repe and mowe / and exclude ydelnesse,
No man sparyd / and husbondys wyl not faylle
To ryse up erly / And calle vp the poraylle,
Blowe ther hornys / or the larke synge,
And Stuff ther grangys / with Corn that they hom brynge.

Bees at midsummer bring honey to their hives, the white lilies spread their leaves widely, beasts feed and shelter under the leaves, in the hot sun the grass withers in the meadow, garlands are made from white and red roses, and everything begins to ripen, as happens also with man with advancing age.

Strawberries and cherries may be seen in the gardens, the beans are ripe, and the pea-pods are green. For fever, when men are sick, people gather purslane and fresh lettuce. In this season Flora, queen of the flowers, changes her bright varied clothes to yellow. The strength of the plants begins to sink down again.

There is no need to linger over this process, but set your inmost heart solely on God. O Alexander, let your heart and thought not change, but thank the Lord for what he has sent. Be content, then, with either poverty or riches, taking pleasure in what God sends, in God alone, and with God as your sufficiency.

For by the teaching of saints and learned men, according to the reckoning up of your deserts, and in accordance with the fruits of your good works you shall be rewarded. This is true and no lie. With peace eternal at the last, at your ending, to reign with Christ in the courts of heaven when, triumphant, you have gained the victory over your enemies.

Then follows after the third season called Autumn

This time customarily makes everyone busy. Each active man gives himself up to work, to reap and mow and avoid idleness. No man can be spared, and husbandmen will not fail to get up early and summon the poor. They blow their horns before the lark begins to sing and fill their barns with the corn that they bring home.

The tyme by processe / voydeth the feeld of greyn,
Takith awey / from braunchys ther swetnesse,
Causeth the trees / of frute to be bareyn,
The levys falle / the wynd abrood hem dresse,
The day, the nyght / bothe of Oon gretnesse,
The sonne in libra / Egal be ballaunce,
As is the wyl / of goddys Ordynaunce.

This sesoun is dredfull / and distemperat,
disposed to feverys / thorough ayr of pestilence,
Offte Chaungyng / and seeld in Oon estat,
Peryllous for syknesse / and with violence;
Off trouble humours / doth folk ful greet offence,
ffor flewme this tyme / hath domynacioun;
Be-war of syknesse / that gynneth in that sesoun.

Erthe, Autumpnus / and Age accordyn in Oon
Slough, malencolye / spatlyng euere Among,
Dul Courbyd dounward / whan myght & lust is goon;
fful of Ire / though he be not strong,
Soone mevyd / wheer it be right or wrong:
And thus senectus / with Autumpne doth accord,
He and this sesoun / drawe bothe be O corde.

Autumpne takith / his leve of seynt Clement,
The tyme dyuerse / and wondir varyable,
With strange passions / sodeynly men schent,
be seknessys / which be unkurable;
And for this sesoun / is unkouth & unstable,
With sodeyn Chaunges / and complexyouns to greve,
Therfore in novembre / he takith his leve.

Wherfore considre / in thyn Estat Royal,
Take the moralite / of Autumpne the sesoun,
how it is appropryd / and in Especial
to the thrydde age / and the complexioun
Off the and me / for short conclusyoun.
Wherefore, O Alysaundre / haue in remembraunce,
Peyse euery thyng / and kepe the in good gouernaunce.

By the process of time the field is cleared of grain, the beauty of the branches is taken from them, the trees become barren of fruit, the leaves fall and the wind drives them about. Day and night are of the same length. The sun is in Libra, equal in the scales, in accordance with God's decree.

This season is to be dreaded: it is not temperate, giving rise to fevers from pestilential air, often changing and seldom stable, dangerous because of sickness, and a time of violence. Troublesome 'humours' do people much damage, for catarrh is dominant at this time. Beware of the sickness that begins in this season.

Earth, Autumn and Age agree together. Sloth, melancholy and spitting are always present. [Man is] feeble and bent when strength and energy are gone, full of anger, although not very strong, soon upset, whether rightly or wrongly. And so old age matches autumn: it and this season are both drawn by the same cord.

Autumn takes its leave of St Clement [23 November]. It is a varied time and remarkably changeable. Men may be suddenly overcome by strange passions, by sickness which cannot be cured; and as this season is unpredictable and unstable with sudden changes, and grievous to [men's] constitutions, it therefore takes its leave in November.

And so consider in your royal state, accept the teaching of the season of autumn, how it is especially appropriate to the third age and the temperament — to conclude briefly — of you and me. And therefore, Alexander, be mindful of and ponder on all these things, and preserve yourself by good management.

The fourthe determynacioun of the foure sesouns of the yeer

Afftir hervest / whan men thresshe shevys,
Sowyn whete / gadre wyntre frute in gardynes,
And somyr trees / be bareyn of ther levys,
Men putte in Celerys / Cowche newe wynes;
must lesyth his name / toward seint martynes
muryly drounke / whan it is through ffyn,
And lastith tyl / the sesoun / of Seint Martyn.

The dayes shorte / the nyghtes wondir longe;
Coold and moyst / of flewme nutrytiff,
Contrary to Estas / the frostys been so stronge.
In Rootys restith / the vertu vegetatyff,
Grene herbys / and braunchys lost ther lyff.
The sonne this sesoun / beeyng in Aquarye,
beestys to the bynne / for stormys dar not tarye.

Thus the foure sesouns / devided of the yeere,
ffirst veer whan phebus / doth in his spere aryse,
The growyng tyme / whan buddys oute appere;
Estas folwyng / whan floures in ther guyse
Sprede on ther stalkys / geyn tytan doth aryse;
Autumpne afftir / which longe doth nat tarye,
And yemps endith / the Ende of ffebruarye.

Thus four tymes / makith vs a merour Cleer
Off mannys lyff / and a ful pleyn ymage.
Ver and Iuuentus / togedir haue sogeer,
Estas folwith / longyng to saddere age;
To vs Autumpne / bryngeth his massage
Off Senectus / Wynter last of alle,
How dethys Orlogge / doth On vs calle.

With veer in youthe / we hadde lustynesse,
Which is inpossyble / ageyn to Recure;
Etas gaff vs strengthe / and hardynesse
fflouryng in ffreshnesse / not longe tendure.
Autumpne afftir / bryngeth vs a ffigure
Off Senectus / Wynter of Crokyd age,
How al thyng passith / halt here no long Ostage.

The fourth and last of the four seasons of the year

After harvest, when men thresh sheaves, sow wheat and gather fruit for the winter in the gardens, and summer trees are bare of their leaves, men lay down new wines in cellars. Must [grape-juice during the process of fermentation in wine-making] loses its name towards St Martin's day [11 November], merrily drunk when it is quite ready.

The days are short, the nights extremely long, the cold and damp are productive of catarrh. In contrast to summer, the frosts are very hard. The sap sinks down to the roots, green plants and branches die off, the sun in this season being in Aquarius. Beasts dare not linger at the manger because of the storms.

Thus of the four seasons into which the year is divided, the first is spring when Phoebus arises in his sphere, the time of growth when buds burst out, summer following as the flowers, in their own way, open on their stems when Titan arises. Autumn comes after but does not tarry long, and winter ends at the end of February.

Thus four periods make us a clear mirror of man's life, and a very plain image of it. Spring and youth together have a short stay. Summer follows, belonging to a more serious age. Autumn brings his message to us of advancing age. Winter last of all [tells] how Death's hourglass calls us [all].

With spring in youth we had [a] liveliness which it is impossible to bring back again. Summer gave us strength and hardihood, flourishing with a freshness not long to endure. Autumn afterwards shows us an image of maturity, winter of crooked age, of how everything passes, and can have no long stay here.

Loo Alisaundre / ye mowne se thynges tweyne,
Avauntyng lying / longyng vnto Age;
Malencoly / fals demyng and disdeyne,
Many passyouns / Rancour and dotage;
Ende of this lyff / terme of our viage:
ffor decrepitus / hath his marke sett,
This world shal ende / it may nat be lett.

Thus to make / a Combynacyoun
Off veer and youthe / be a manere accordaunce
Off mannys sadnesse / and Estas the sesoun
fflouring in lust / tyme of most plesaunce,
Autumpne and eld / with ther greet haboundaunce.
Thanne folwith wyntir / and al doth ovir caste:
So doth age for it / may not alwey laste.

Off this forseyd / take the morallite,
Settith asyde / alle materys spooke in veyn;
The foure sesouns / shewe in ther degre,
ffirst veer and Estas / next Autumpne with his greyn,
Constreynt of wyntir / with frostys ovir leyn,
To oure foure Ages / the sesouns wel applyed;
deth al consumyth / which may nat be denyed.

From Lydgate and Burgh's *Secrees of old Philisoffres*, a Version of the
Secreta Secretorum, ed. Robert Steele for the Early English Text Society,
London 1894, lines 1296-1491.

So, Alexander, you must contemplate two things: boasting and lying belong to old age, with melancholy, impaired judgment and scornfulness, many passions, rancour and senility; and the end of this life, the conclusion of our journey, for decrepitude has set its limit. This world will end; it cannot be prevented.

So to bring together spring and youth in terms of their similarity; of man's seriousness and the season of summer, flowering in delight, the time of most pleasure; autumn and maturity with their great abundance; after which follows winter and overcasts all, as does age, for [life] cannot last for ever.

Of all this that has been said accept the lesson, put aside all matters unprofitably spoken. The four seasons show each in its degree — first spring and summer, next autumn with its grain, [then] the constraints of winter, subject to frosts — that the seasons may be well applied to our four ages. Death consumes everything — which cannot be denied.

FOUR

The Arming of the Warrior

Erec is armed by Enide

Erec was eager for the battle, so he asks for arms and they are given to him. The maiden herself puts on his arms (though she casts no spell or charm), laces on his iron greaves, and makes them fast with thongs of deer-hide. She puts on his corslet with its strong meshes, and laces on his ventail. The gleaming helmet she sets upon his head, and thus arms him well from tip to toe. At his side she fastens his sword, and then orders his horse to be brought, which is done. Up he jumped clear of the ground. The damsel then brings the shield and the strong lance; she hands him the shield and he takes it and hangs it about his neck by the strap. She has placed the lance in his hand and he has grasped it by the butt.

From Chrétien's *Erec et Enide* in *Arthurian Romances*, translated by W.W. Comfort (1914), p. 10.

On a subsequent occasion Erec is armed again

Then Erec summoned another squire and bade him bring his arms with which to arm his body. Then he went up into a bower, and had a Limoges rug laid out before him on the floor. Meanwhile, the squire ran to fetch the arms and came back and laid them on the rug. Erec took a seat opposite, on the figure of a leopard which was portrayed on the rug. He prepares and gets ready to put on his arms: first, he had laced on a pair of greaves of polished steel; next, he dons a hauberk, which was so fine that not a mesh could be cut away from it. This hauberk of his was rich indeed, for neither inside nor outside of it was there enough iron to make a needle, nor could it gather any rust; for it was all made of worked silver in tiny meshes triple-wove; and it was made with such skill that I can assure you that no one who had put it on would have been more uncomfortable or sore because of it, than if he had put on a silk jacket over his undershirt. The knights and squires all began to wonder why he was being armed; but no-one dared ask him why. When they had put on his hauberk, a valet laces about his head a helmet fluted with a band of gold, shining brighter than a mirror. Then he takes the sword and girds it on, and orders them to bring him saddled his bay steed of Gascony.

From *Erec et Enide*, op. cit., pp. 34–5.

King Arthur arms himself

After evensong, Sir Arthur himself went to his wardrobe and took off his clothes, armed himself in an acton with very rich gold embroidery, with, on top of that, a jeryne made at Acre, then a light coat of armour of very fine mail, and a close-fitting tunic of Ierodyne slashed at the edge. He puts on a helmet of burnished silver, the best in Basille, with splendid borders, the crest and the crown adorned with clasps of bright gold set with stones; the visor and the mouthpiece fashioned most beautifully, free of any defect, with airholes in the silver. His gauntlets were brightly gilded and chased at the borders with beading and embossed ornaments glorious in colour. He puts a broad shield on his arm and asks for his sword, goes to his stirrup and strides into the saddle, exerts himself powerfully and moves gracefully. He spurs his bay steed and rides to the wood, where his knights awaited him in very good order.

From the Alliterative *Morte Arthure*, ed. cit., lines 900–919.

The arming of the Black Prince

He went down to the bank [of the brook] and stayed there a while until he was armed and equipped in the very best way. The lower part of his legs was covered with steel, with the armour for his chest and belly brightly polished. He had arm-guards of burnished steel, closely woven, with plate-armour fastened at the back to protect his body. He put on a well-fitting doublet, joined at the sides, and a broad escutcheon at the back, with another on his breast, with the three feathers as well, worked in the same way, and bound round with gold wire.

From *Winner and Waster*, ed. Sir Israel Gollancz, Cambridge 1974, lines 109–118,

The arming of Sir Thopas

He dide next his white leere
Of cloth of lake fyn and cleere,
   A breech and eek a sherte;
And next his sherte an aketoun,
And over that an haubergeoun
   For percynge of his herte;

And over that a fyn hawberk,
Was al ywroght of Jewes werk,
   Ful strong it was of plate;
And over that his cote-armour
As whit as is a lilye flour,
   In which he wol debate.

His sheeld was al of gold so reed,
And therinne was a bores heed,
   A charbocle bisyde;
And there he swoor on ale and breed
How that the geaunt shal be deed,
   Bityde what bityde!

His jambeux were of quyrboilly,
His swerdes shethe of yvory,
   His helm of latoun bright;
His sadel was of rewel boon,
His brydel as the sonne shoon,
   Or as the moone light.

His spere was of fyn ciprees,
That bodeth werre, and nothyng pees,
   The heed ful sharpe ygrounde;
His steede was al dappull gray,

It gooth an ambil in the way
  Ful softely and rounde
    In londe.

Chaucer, *Sir Thopas*, *The Canterbury Tales*, ed. cit., lines 857–87.

'To arme a man', from a fifteenth-century manuscript

First ye must set on sabbatons and tie them upon the shoes with small laces so that they will bend; and then greaves; and then cuisses; and then the breech of mail; and then the tonlets; then the breastplate; then the vambraces; then the rerebraces; then the gloves. Then hang his dagger upon his side; then his short sword on the left side in a round ring, all naked to pull it out lightly. Then put his coat upon his back, and then his basinet pinned upon two great staples before the breastplate, with a double buckle behind upon the back, in order to make the helmet sit correctly; and then his long sword in his hand; then his pennant in his hand, painted with Saint George or with Our Lady, to bless him as he goes towards the field and in the field.

Dillon, 'On a MS Collection of Ordinances of Chivalry of the Fifteenth Century, Belonging to Lord Hastings,' *Archaeologia*, LVII (1900), 43–4, in *Chaucer's World*, compiled by Edith Rickert, London and New York, 1948, p. 156.

FIVE

Gawain's Arrival at the Castle

Gawain reaches the Grail castle

He gazed far along the riverbank, and then suddenly saw
something to cheer him, for just at the edge of a forest he caught a
glimpse of a tower, and it was huge and tall. I have Chrétien to
vouch for that, who was full of praise for the fortress. Gawain set
off towards it at once, happier now and greatly cheered. He rode
on until he reached the gate – it was not closed – and did not
delay, but dismounted immediately. More than a hundred boys
appeared, all eager to serve him, and gave his mount to the
master of the stables who provided him with oats and hay. Then
they led Sir Gawain to be disarmed in an antechamber: and from
there to Limoges there was none so rich and beautiful, paved
with marble and strewn with fresh grass. They brought him a
brand new gown lined with grey and white fur, and Gawain,
who proved his worth in all knightly deeds, took it and donned it
straight away. And then, without the slightest delay, the boys led
him from the chamber to the hall. There was nothing pale about
Gawain's looks; and as soon as he was robed he followed the
boys into the hall.

From Chrétien de Troyes, *Perceval: the Story of the Grail*, The First
Continuation, ed. cit., Cambridge 1982, pp. 110-11.

Gawain is welcomed at the castle of the Widowed Lady

The lady bade the boy take Sir Gawain's horse into the castle, while she led him up to the hall, where his arms were laid aside and water was brought for him to wash his face and hands, for he had been bruised by his hauberk. Then the lady had him robed in a rich gown of silk and gold, lined with ermine, and then left the chamber and bade Sir Gawain be seated beside her.

From *The High Book of the Grail: A translation of the thirteenth century romance of Perlesvaus*, ed. cit., p. 44.

SIX

The Hunt

Arthur hunts the deer

Arthur eagerly rides with his nobles to set them at their hunting-stations, the truth to tell; he assigned them their hunting stations, to tell you the truth. At once each lord without delay took his place by an oak with his bow and his hunting dog, under the boughs.

These brave warriors waited under the boughs to speed their arrows at the barren does on the bare hills. The men could soon see the herds and hear the hunt with its horns in the leafless wood. They uncouple their hounds by the cold cliffs and pet their little dogs to keep them calm. Great numbers of the female deer were killed. With many lively hounds they closely pursue them, with many forays and much slaughter both in the woods and on the hills. In the hollows all the deer lie concealed, motionless with fear.

Then the deer hide in the dark woods, and in terror of death the doe cowers. By the swift-flowing water that dashes by with a rushing sound they make war on the wild beasts and work them woe. The hunters shout among the hillocks and cliffs and hurry to their hunting-stations, unleashing fresh hounds on the roe-deer. They had no mercy on any game whatsoever, as the huge greyhounds went so eagerly through the thickets. The king blows his horn to assemble the hounds and follows fast on the trail with a great crowd of hunt-servants to see that fine sight.

From *The Awntyrs off Arthure at the Terne Wathelyn*, ed. Ralph Hanna III, Manchester University Press 1974, lines 33–65.

Tristrem shows how to cut up a deer

The forest was beautiful, and extensive, and full of wild beasts. The courtiers were close to it; while the palmers guided him to it. Tristrem sees the hunters riding, leading leashes of hounds; they took at that time some fat harts that fed in the field. Tristrem was dressed in 'blehand' [a kind of cloth] – the hunters saw him.

They cut up and carried off the beasts, quartering them as if they were cattle slaughtered at Martinmas for winter provision, that had been bought by husbandmen. Tristrem then spoke to them, saying that he thought it extraordinary:

'I never before saw such wild beasts so carelessly dealt with. If I know anything at all about it, you are ruining them by your foolishness.'

Up stood a bold servant and replied to Tristrem:

'We and our ancient forebears have always advocated this. You have suggested another way. Over there lies an unflayed beast: dress it in your way, and we will gladly watch you on the spot.'

As the tradition has it, the hunters all watched him. Tristrem cut open the breast, the tongue lay next the spleen; he with great delight cut out the hemings [a piece of the hide cut out to make brogues for the huntsmen] and laid it aside. He pressed down the breech, cut it off, and dressed it. After that he at once boldly cut off the skin. He then dressed the beasts, as many beasts have since been dressed. The shoulder was the first breadth. He quickly took out the bowels. He went to the knees and cut them right in two. He adjusted all the small guts, he set aside the paunch, he gave away the numbles as a reward. Those that were there saw that in that very manner. Further, he cut the backbone crosswise, he cut the chine in two. He gave the left shoulder to the forester as his rights, along with the heart, liver, lights, and blood for the quarry. He sets the dogs on the hide; he let them all see. In due order, he gave its gifts to the raven which sat on the forked tree. 'Hunters, where are you? You should blow the tokening.' He tied the paunch and also the *gargiloun* to the *tinde*. They blew in the right manner, and sounded the proper call.

From *Sir Tristrem*, ed. George P. McNeill, Edinburgh and London 1886, lines 441–510. Lines 474–510 are given in the editor's translation.

From the Book of St Albans

This book contains a treatise on hunting by Dame Julians Barnes, probably the wife of the holder of the manor of Julians Barnes near St Albans.

'How ye shall breeke[1] an hert[2]'

And for to speke of the hert, while we thynke oon,
My chylde, fyrst ye shall serve when he shall be undoon[3],
And that is for to say, or ever ye him dyght[4],
Within his owne hornys to lay hym upright.
At th'essay[5] cut hym, that lordys may see
Anoon fat or leen wheder that he bee.
Than cut of[f] the coddis[6] the bely even froo,
Or ye begynne hym to flee[7], and then shall ye goo
At chaulis[8] to begynne, assone as ye may,
And slyttith hym downe even to th'assay,
And fro th'assay even downe the bele shall ye slitt
To the pissill[9], ther the codde was away kytt.
Then slit the lyfte legge even first before
And then the lyfte legge byhynde, or ye do moore,
And thees oder legges uppon the right syde
Uppon thessame maner slyt ye that tyde.
To goo to the chekys[10] looke ye be prest,
And so fleeth hym downe even to the brest,
And so fleeth hym forth right unto th'essay,
Even to the place where the codde was cut away,
Then fleeth thessame wyse all that oder syde,
Bot let the tayll of the beest still ther oon byde.
Then shall ye hym undo, my chylde, I yow rede,
Ryght uppon his awne skynne, and lay hit on brede[11].
Take heede of the cuttyng of thessame dere,
And begynne fyrst to make the erbere[12],

---

1 *breeke*, cut up.   2 *hert*, applied to a deer from his sixth year.   3 *undoon*, cut up.
4 *dyght*, prepare.   5 *essay*, assay, breast of a deer.   6 *coddis*, testicles.   7 *flee*, flay.   8 *chaulis*, jaws.   9 *pissill*, penis.   10 *chekys*, cheeks, jaws.   11 *brede*, bread.   12 *erbere*, the gullet or first stomach of ruminants.

Then take owt the shulderis, and slyttith anoon
The baly to the syde from the corbyn bone[13].
  That is corbyn's[14] fee,
  At the deeth he will be.

Then take owt the sewet, that hit be not lafte,
For that, my chylde, is good for lechecraft[15].
Than put thyn honde softely under the brest bone,
And ther shall ye take owt th'erber anoon.
Than put owt the paunche, and from the paunche taas[16]
Away wightly[17] the rate[18], sich as he haas.
Hoole[19] it with a fyngre, do as I yow kenne[20],
And with the bloode and the grece fillith hit thenne.
Looke threde that ye have and nedell therto
For to sew it with all, or ye moore do.
The smale guttis than ye shall owt pyt,
From hem take the maw[21], foryet not it.
Than take owt the lever[22], and lay hit on the skynne,
And after that the bledder withowt moore dynne.
Then dresse the nombles[23] first, that ye reke.
Downe the avauncers[24] kerve, that cleven to the necke,
And downe with the bolthrote[25] put them anoon,
And kerve up the flesh ther up to the hach[26] boon,
And so forth the fillittis[27], that ye up arere[28],
That fallith to the nombles and shall be ther
With the neres[29] also and sewit that ther is
Even to the mydryf that uppon hym is.
Than take downe the mydrif from the sides hoote,
And heve up the nombles hoole by the boll throte.
In thyn hond than them holde, and looke and se
That all that longith them to togeder that thay be,
Than take them to thy broder[30] to holde for trist[31]
Whylis thow them dowbyst[32] and dightis, as the list[33],

---

13 *corbyn bone*, pelvic bone. **14** *corbyn*, raven. **15** *lechecraft*, remedy. **16** *taas*, take. **17** *wightly*, nimbly. **18** *rate*, spleen. **19** *hoole*, make a hole in. **20** *kenne*, teach. **21** *maw*, stomach. **22** *lever*, liver. **23** *nombles*, inward parts of the deer. **24** *avauncers*, foremost part of the deer's numbles, flesh that covers the deer's gullet. **25** *bolthrote*, larynx, throat. **26** *hach bone*, backbone, spine. **27** *fillittis*, fillets. **28** *arere*, lift up, raise. **29** *neres*, kidneys. **30** *broder*, comrade, companion. **31** *for trist*, in trust. **32** *dowbyst*, prepare. **33** *as the list*, as you please.

Than [take] away the lyghtis[34], and oon the skynne them lay
To abyde the querre[35], my chylde, I yow pray.

Than shall ye slyt the slough[36] ther as the hert lith,
And take away the eres[37] from it and by slyth[38],
For sich heris hath his hert ay it uppon,
As men may se in the beest when he is undon.
And in the myddis of the hert a boon shall ye fynde,
Looke ye yeve hit to a lorde and chylde be kynde,
For hit is kynde[39] for mony malydies,
And in the myddis of the hert evermore it lies.
Than shall ye kyt the skyrtis[40] the teeth even fro,
And after the ragge[41] boon cuttis even also
The forchis[42] and the sydes even betwene,
And looke that yowre knyfe[s] ay whettyd bene.
Than turne up the forchis, and frote[43] them with bloode
For to save the grece, so do men of goode[44].
Than shall ye cut the nek the sydes even fro,
And the hede fro the nek cuttyth also,
The toong, the brayn, the paunch and the necke.
When thay wash[en] be weell with water of the becke[45],
The smale guttis to the lightis, in the derys
Above the hert of the beest when thow them reris,
With all the blode that ye may gete and wyn,
All togeder shall be take and layde oon the skyn
To geve yowre houndes. That callid is, I wis,
The quyrre, above the skyn for it etyn is.
And who dightis hym so by my counsayle
Shall have the lefte shuder[46] for hys travayle,
And the right shulder, where so ever he bee,
Yeveth to the foster, for that is his fee,
And the lyver also of thessame beest
To the fosterys knave yeveth at the leest.
The nombles trussith in the skynne, and hardell[47] hem fast,

---

34 *lyghtis*, lungs. **35** *querre, quyrre*, parts of the deer given to the hounds on the deer's skin. **36** *slough*, skin or membrane enclosing and covering the heart of the deer. **37** *eres, heris*, auricles of the heart. **38** *slyth*, skilfulness. **39** *kynde*, good for. **40** *skyrtis*, rim of the lips and mouth or nose of a deer (considered a delicacy). **41** *ragge*, sternal bone. **42** *forchis*, clavicles of a deer. **43** *frote*, rub. **44** *men of goode*, men of property, rank and standing. **45** *becke*, brook. **46** *shuder*, shoulder. **47** *hardell*, tie with supple branches.

The sides and the forches togeder, that thay last,
With th'ender legges, be doon so it shall.
Then bryng it hoom and the skynne with all
The nombles and the hornes. At the lordis yate
Then boldely blow the price[48] tharat
   Yowre play for to mynne[49],
   Or that ye come inne.

From *Cynegetica XI. Julians Barnes: Boke of Huntyng*. Edition critique
publiée avec une traduction en Français moderne par Gunnar Tilande,
Karlshamn 1964, lines 543–640.

---

48 *blow the price*, blow the horn at the lord's gate when the deer has been killed
and brought home. **49** *play for to mynne*, to record your hunting.

Arthur hunts a ferocious boar

The king called to three knights – he himself would be the fourth. He said:

'No more of my household shall go after the boar.'

Both Kay and Gawain and Baldwin of Britain, the huntsman and the master of hounds, made themselves ready very quickly. The king armed himself in haste, and with him those three men. Now all four are quite ready and are setting out.

Into the forest they go, those men who were strong and noble. The hunter to the north began to blow his bugle, He uncoupled the small hounds as he well knew how to do. Eagerly they ran southwards, the hounds with their open mouths running in a pack. They found the scent of the boar and swiftly pursued him. When he heard them he cautiously withdrew to his lair and struck them down fiercely, fighting very ferociously. But you can be quite sure, sirs, he felt little fear.

They held him fast in his den. He cut the bold hounds to pieces, both young and old, and put an end to them. The hounds came running up to him and fearlessly brought him to bay but not one was so strong that he dare seize the fiend. Then the hunter said,

'Look at him there! You have no need to seek him further. Now you can soon get at him. Let's see who does best! You need look no further for him, as I value my life – unless he kills all four of you, that terrible enemy!'

Then the hunter makes for home again. The king calls to Sir Gawain and to Baldwin of Britain and to bold Kay. He said:

'Sirs, in your company I make this vow, that however strong he is I will attack this fiend, cut him to pieces and finish him off, without any assistance, if I survive until tomorrow morning. And now, sirs, I command you to do as I have just done. Each one of you make your vow.'

They readily agree.

Gawain, Kay and Baldwin all make vows which do not involve the boar-hunt and go off in different directions, leaving Arthur to deal with the beast on his own.

To speak first of our king – as one naturally does – from the beginning, of how he carried out his intention: as he looked at his hounds the boar with his enormous shoulders rushed after him in the field, rapidly working havoc. Then the king shouted, calling out the hunting-terms to encourage his hounds, and rode up on his horse. As soon as he got there the boar dashed at him: he never before saw such a sight. It caused him to be greatly alarmed.

He was afraid and apprehensive of the fierce, strong beast. The boar began to roar and rumble and come on with gaping jaws. No-one could see his lair for the hounds and slain men that he had drawn to his den and stripped to the bones. Then he whetted his tusks so as to attack the king. Without stopping, he tears up tree-trunks and rocks. He begins to root about in his rage, he tears up many a root with his three-foot long tusks, so furiously he rages.

Then the king seizes his spear to bear down upon that boar, but no threat can frighten him, so tough was his hide. The huge long spear-shaft flew all to splinters, while the fine horse that was so strong had fallen to the ground. When he saw his chance, he gave the king such a blow before he could seize his bridle that he could feel it ever afterwards. His horse was struck stark dead so that he never moved from the spot. The king offered up a prayer to Jesus to protect him in that peril.

Then the king freeing himself from his saddle quickly got on his feet. He prays to St Margaret to guard him in his peril. He acted as a brave knight, drew his bright sword and raised his shield on high, for his spear was broken. Then he swiftly went – rapidly without more ado – to attack the fiend with his hideous bristles. So they encountered in the field with all the weapons that he could wield, but the boar shattered the shield that he bore on his breast.

He kneels down there and prays to Him who is so gracious, 'Send me victory! This fiend is pursuing me.'
The boar grew more enraged, snorted and rolled his eyes, smelling vilely like a malt-furnace or a kitchen. The king could not see him, but he crouched down by a tree, so revolted was he by the smell and the stench. And as the boar came close to the oak the king struck him fiercely so that he was stunned. He gets the upper hand.

Thus he gains the advantage with tremendous blows. Strong though he was, that fierce beast had to pause. The king with his noble sword met the boar coming towards him. Right up to the hilt of his sword he runs full tilt, so that it went in at the throat. The boar had no joy of that encounter: he began to stagger and reel from the injury he had received. He sinks down in agony. The king was ready to cut him up and sever his two broad shoulders.

The king understood the huntsman's art. He cut out the neck very skilfully. He set the head of that fierce beast on a stake. After that he cuts up the best of the game in the forest, hanging both the strips and the slices on the oak. He kneels down there in his love for Her who is so gracious and says,

'This help Thou hast sent me for Thy Son's sake!'

Though he was in a deep dale he had no knight to guard him, but exhausted, he fell asleep: he could no longer stay awake.

The Avowing of Arthur, lines 69–272.
From *Middle English Metrical Romances*, vol. II, edited by W.H. French and C.B. Hale, New York 1964.

Guy of Warwick hunts the boar

They enturde into a wylde foreste
And there they fonde a bore wylde and preste.
All the howndys, they had, than
Aftur the bore faste they ranne.
The bore awey faste ys gone
And many of the howndys he hath slone:
Moo, then twenty, in a stownde
Had he broght vnto the grownde.
He passyd the foreste hastelye:
They folowed hym wyth grete crye.
Faste he passyd thorow the londe:
Ther durste no hownde come nerehonde.
The knyghtys prekyd aftur faste,
Tyll ther horsys myght not laste.
The howndys, that folowed that day,
Were slayne all be the way:
Thes odur were werye,
They wente home, they myght not drye,
All, but thre, that were wyght,
That folowed alwey wyth ther myght,
Tyll they come to Bretayne.
Ther folowed them nodur knyght nor swayne:
Of them all was no huntere,
That wyst, where the borre were,
But syr Gye hymselfe allone,
That folowed faste wyth grete randone
On hys stede faste prykynge
And wyth hys horne faste blowynge.
　Gye chasyd the borre so faste,
He came to Bretayne at the laste.
Be then was the boore full hote:
He fonde a dyke and yn he smote.
There he wandyrde faste abowte
And wrotyd faste wyth hys snowte.
Gye sawe the bore well
And, what he dud, euery delle.
Downe he lyght of hys stede
And to the bore soon he yede.

He toke hys swyrde in hys hande:
The boore hym sye and came rennande.
Gye on the rygge smote hym soo,
That hys body felle in twoo.
The boore felle downe at the laste,
And Gye wyth hys horne blewe a blaste.
He wende to haue had some felowe,
But ther was none, that dud hym knowe.
He was in a farre cuntre
All aloone fro hys meyne,
And, as he openyd there the boore,
Euyr he blewe more and more.

From *The Romance of Guy of Warwick*, ed. Dr Julius Zupitza, Early English Text Society, 1885-6, lines 6417-66.

SEVEN

The Temptation Theme

From the Story of Yder

Yder, a young squire, successfully resists temptation, strengthened by
his devotion to his lady, and so wins his spurs.

Yder met a king in full armour, just as he had passed a wood. The
king's name was Ivenant, and he was a brave and courteous
knight. Yder greeted him and stopped, and so the king asked him
which way he was going.

'I am looking for an adventure, my lord, as a knight should do,'
he said.

'You have found one,' the king replied. 'Do you see this
beautiful armour of mine? Would you like to win this?'

'I should like to very much indeed,' Yder answered. So the king
said to him:

'I offer this armour to you, but it must be on one condition. This
broad road will take you where you will see a castle of mine. Wait
for me in the hall. I think that you will find my wife there. No
man can defend himself against her: she makes him accept her
love, so that he does not win the armour easily. Of this I am quite
certain, that she will never love anyone but me. It amuses me and
gives me pleasure to offer all my armour to every squire I meet.
And so I have made an agreement with you. If you are seduced
you will be made to look a fool.'

'Seduced, by God!' Yder said to himself. 'I shall not lose my
heart to her, when she begins the dance.'

This was because he was thinking of his own beloved. He
agreed to the bargain with the king. Then the king said to him:

95

'Go straight to the castle and await me there. I am going to the perilous ford and shall be with you again immediately afterwards. Then you will see the master in his castle.'

Then he left the young man.

Now Yder was without a guide, but he was a young knight and so it was quite impossible that any woman, other than the one who possessed his heart, should please him – he would never love anyone else. Yder came to the castle and dismounted near the hall. There, in the gravel, was a fountain, under a laurel in the courtyard, the pebbles of which were beautifully white. He tied his horse to a branch and then went up the steps to the palace. There were many knights, ladies and squires on the dais and in various places playing chess and other games. There was a great noise and a great deal of shouting, but he lay down on a soft chair, for it was a long time since he had slept. What with the noise that he could hear, what with his love-longing, what with the strain of it, and all the weeping and all the watching, sleep soon seized the young man. He folded his cloak under his head, and desired nothing better than this bed, in which he lay with the utmost content.

The queen was in her own room. She called a servant, for it was very hot and she was overcome with the heat.

'Go to the fountain which springs up by the laurel down there in the courtyard,' she said. 'I want to cool my feet in its water, so hurry up and come back.'

Her feet were very hot; so the girl took a silver bowl, went straight out from the room and came into the hall. She saw Yder who lay sleeping, came right up to him, and stopped. She did not know him, and she wanted to find out about him. She was so intent on looking at him, his shapely legs, his beautiful feet, his hands, his arms, his sides, his eyes, his neck, his head and his face, that she forgot what she was supposed to be doing. The fountain was quite forgotten. She was thinking of something else. She was away from the room for a long time, which she was sorry for, for the lady would reprove her, and she had only herself to blame. (It often happens that a very sensible lady, when she has a silly maid, is exasperated by her stupidity.) She came back to the room, and her lady was much annoyed when she saw that her bowl was empty. The maid had forgotten all about it and so was just holding it. The lady asked her where the water was, and the maid was completely dumbfounded.

'Good heavens!' she said, 'I haven't got a drop!'

'Haven't you?' said the lady. 'And why haven't you?'

And she replied, 'I've forgotten it.'

'Then you'll pay for it on your skin. What were you looking for out there?'

An old woman who was the housekeeper said:

'She ought to pay for it. I'll beat her now on her bare skin!'

'If I am beaten for it,' answered the maid, 'I shall be beaten because of a young man, and I don't think I've ever seen one more beautiful.'

When the queen heard what she said she asked her,

'Where is he, idiot?'

'In this palace,' she answered, 'asleep with his head on a bench, and I repeat that I have never seen anyone so beautiful.'

The queen took a cloak of silken cloth, of grey material. She was without her head-dress, and without her shift, too, because it was hot. She left her room and hurried to the place where Yder lay. When she had looked at him for a while, she put her arm around his neck, and touched his face with her cheek. Yder sat up instantly, but however much he tried to draw back, she still held on to him.

'Friend,' she said, 'where have you come from? You seem to me to be very disdainful.'

'I was born in Carlisle,' he said, 'and I am disdainful when I want to be.'

'You must have spoken to the king' she said, 'and so don't be so ill-mannered and contemptuous to me, because I love you to distraction. You seem to me to be quite the most handsome young man that I've ever seen. My lord makes this agreement about his armour with the passers-by. He shames me for his amusement, but I acquit you of all shame, because the matter concerns only myself. And do not be at all alarmed about it. You will never possess his armour, but I have much better armour that you shall have, and a good horse and a rich suit of clothes too. So I offer you myself and my love, and I want to be sure of you.'

'I don't care anything for you and your love,' he said, 'because I should not value it in the very least.'

'Should not value it?' she said. 'Good heavens!'

'Yes, you are the wife of the king. He is handsome and good, and I am a mere boy. I am not worth a hundredth part of him. Out of sheer lust and stupidity you are trying to extort love from someone who is worth much less than the man you already possess. But you are very wicked in this, if someone other than he can really please you. I should be making a mockery of him when he was expecting to find loyal love. Loyal love does not even know how to change. You are not in its power – not you, nor anyone else who has a changeable heart. Loyal love demands a steadfast heart. You would have taken and changed it completely; you would have made a completely new bargain. Love has its merchants; but noble lovers never find that love avenges itself sharply, because they live in hope.'

'Friend,' she said, 'you speak the truth. If you wish to have my love, I will love you loyally.'

And Yder briefly told her that she lied, and that he wanted nothing to do with her love, and he began to pull himself up, and she tried to stop him doing it. He pushed against her as much as he could, while she was pulling him down all the time. Yder gave her a kick in the stomach so that she fell on her back in front of him, and in consequence she became quite livid with anger. I do not know how she got up again because he would not let her get up. The lady became quite pale. The people who were playing games in the hall saw the blow and commented on it, laughing a great deal, and much enjoying it, for they were very well acquainted with the custom. One nudged another with his elbow, but they did not look round at all. They paid attention to their games and pretended that they were concentrating on their sport, and immensely enjoying themselves.

The queen got up, and did not dare to touch Yder again.

'You lout,' she said, 'you are much too rough. But one thing I do ask you for the sake of whoever you most love, that as soon as you have the armour that I am sure that you are going to receive, you will at least speak a few words to me.'

Yder said to her:

'I promise you that I will.'

The queen went away, extremely angry and much hurt, for she knew very well that she had been made to look very foolish, being rejected in such a way by Yder. So then the king returned. The knights rose from the dais and took off his armour there in the hall, and the king asked them about the young man, and if they had seen him. They replied that he was in the hall, and then one of them told the king on behalf of them all, that Yder had defended himself with valour – much joy had the queen had of him! They had heard what she said to him and the answer that he gave her. She kissed him, but he pushed her off, called her a stupid whore, and did not even take her hand and hold it. He gave her such a kick that she fell over on the floor.

'As you promised him the armour and made the agreement with him which you have made with the others, prepare the gift that he has been told of, for you can justly offer it to him.'

'Send him here,' said the king; and he was brought before him.

'Young man,' he said, 'it was a bad bargain I made with you, that I should give you my armour. Now you are going to get it, it seems to me.'

He replied, 'Sir, if you keep the bargain that you made with me, I am well aware that it is your duty to do so.'

'You would be much mistaken if you were to fear that I should not keep to my bargain. I acquit myself of that: come forward.'

Yder was very light-hearted and joyful now, but he was by no means forgetful (for love would not let him forget) that he had a duty to speak to the queen because she had begged him to, for the sake of the person that he loved most. He asked leave of the king to go and speak with her, and the king graciously gave it. He briefly said to the knights that his armour should remain there. But of all those who heard him, there was not one there who was not sorry.

Yder had no intention of going in when he reached her room, because he did not want to be guilty of any misdemeanour. He spoke loudly so that the king could hear him. The queen called, and he replied that he wished to receive his armour from the king, but that his agreement with her obliged him to delay. The queen said to him:

'Friend, you have certainly taken good advice.'

Yder replied, 'I have had very good advice; and so I have come to you for this reason only, that I had promised you that I would. I cannot see you, but I can hear you, and I have no desire ever to see you again. And so I leave you for the silly woman that you are.'

The king laughed at this when he heard it, and all the knights too. Yder then came straight to the king, and he armed him in his own armour, then gave him the accolade when he had girded him with his sword, as was the ancient custom; even in our time they do no more. He was well armed, for nothing was lacking, and the king made him mindful of great deeds and filled his heart with the hope that he would be of great prowess. When the king had armed Yder he took him to the chapel and they both made their way to the altar, Yder remaining beside him while mass was sung.

Yder placed his sword on the altar and offered and presented it to God, redeeming it with the thirteen pence, and then took leave of the chaplain; and the king took him by the hand until they came to the door of the chapel, where the man who was holding his war-horse was. The king and the man who was with him requested him to mount. He did not need to vault from the stirrup, but sprang into the saddle from the ground; he took his good shield and strong lance. Then he spurred the splendid horse and galloped through the courtyard, managing him beautifully and riding well. He turned him well and held him in skilfully, took a turn around and then came back. He leant on his lance and asked leave to go. But if the king could have kept him by anything that he could think of to offer him, he would never have let him go. Yder said goodbye to the king, commended him and all his household to God, thanked him heartily for making him a knight, saluted him, and went on his way.

From *Yder. Der Iderroman*, ed. H. Gelzer, Dresden 1913, lines 185–510.

How Lancelot was tempted by a beautiful girl sent by Morgan le Fay

That night Lancelot spent in the forest, and when he had lain down, the lady came to him and said:

'Sir knight, stay here.'

'Why, lady?' said he.

'Because,' said she, 'I want to sleep with you.'

And he replied that he would not sleep with her. And she said that he should and he replied that he would not, and that whatever happened he would lie quite alone in his bed. Then he jumped out in his shirt and breeches. And when she saw him she said:

'Sir, now do not be angry, but speak to me on the understanding that I will not touch you if it does not really please you. But now give me a reason as knights ought to do to a lady.'

'I have never done any wrong or villainy to a woman or a girl, and I shall not begin with you.'

'Sir,' said she, 'thank you. But you know well that it is established through all the realm of Logres that if a lady or a girl ask help from a knight, he ought to succour and help her, or he will have lost all his honour. And I beg you that you will help me, now that I have need.'

'What is that?' said Lancelot.

'It is to lie with me,' she said.

'Are you a lady?' he said. 'To my mind you are not, because you seem too bold. And even if a knight asked such a thing of you, and you loved him above all else, he ought not to hear such words from you. Wickedly do you make your request for love-making to a brave knight. Nevertheless, I cannot think you so foolish tonight as to be able to believe that you are saying this to me seriously. You are wanting to test me. And since you are ill-mannered, not evilly disposed towards me, I do not wish to be ill-natured in my reply.'

'I beg you,' she said, 'that you will help me in the greatest need of you that I ever had. I only ask that you will do it for me immediately. And if you fail me in this, I shall consider you to have failed and to be vanquished, for the custom demands it.'

And Lancelot said to her, 'Evil be to him who established this custom and to whoever may uphold it. And I should consider myself defeated, if I were to do this for you.'

'Now you lie down,' said the lady, 'and since you consider it shame and disgrace I shall not lie down with you.'

And he lay down and she threw herself down beside him in the bed and took hold of him tightly by the shirt that he had on. And she drew him to her and acted as if she was dying to kiss him, and when he found that she held him so close, he took her by the two hands and put her down on the ground and held her there so firmly that she could not do anything. And she began to cry and said that she was very ill.

'And I pray you,' she said, 'for God's sake that you will do one thing for me that I ask you, which will not be at all against your honour.'

'I will do it gladly,' he said. 'Tell it me.'

'Willingly,' said she, 'in your ear.'

And he came close to her, and she brought her mouth close and kissed him. And he jumped up so furious, that he all but lost his senses, and ran for his sword, and said to her that if she had not been a woman he would have cut off her head, and she said to him:

'So it seems,' and ran towards him.

And he rushed away out of the pavilion and spat and wiped his mouth very vigorously. And she who had sent him rushing out ran after him and he told her – swearing and vowing it – that he would never return to her. And he went back with great reluctance and lay down in his bed. And the girl lay down elsewhere as if she had never done anything to tempt him.

From *The Vulgate Version of the Arthurian Romances* ed. H.O. Sommer, Washington, D.C., 1908–13, iv, p. 127.

From Hunbaut

Visiting a castle with Hunbaut, Gawain spends the night with his host's beautiful daughter.

'We shall stay overnight, sir, at a castle where the host is not at all the sort that is to the liking of everyone,' Hunbaut said to Gawain.

'He is very rich in gold and silver and he is also lord of a great estate. He shows great anger to anyone who infringes his orders; if a man does not do just as he orders him immediately, then he is forcibly hanged by the neck without respite and without relief. Because his castles are indeed very strong, he fears neither count nor king. He is so proud and so very wicked, and thus it pleases him to commit such outrages as to destroy a good man, or on a very small pretext, to hang a man. But in whatever place he may be, he knows well enough how to spend his own. Make sure that you always remember what I have informed you of. If you wish to know how to behave at his table, severely restrain yourself, because if he does not really take to you, you will repent of it tomorrow, for every day you will be weaker. Let us both fast tomorrow, because a man must indeed fast who cannot have anything to eat, or any earthly possession in this world. For we shall not find anything here until Wednesday – from Tuesday until Wednesday we shall not find anything fit to eat here, either raw or cooked, I am sure; for in this forest where no-one lives, in this land where no-one dwells, where God keeps us, we shall have to pass two very long, hard days. And so I told you before, because I wanted you to be forewarned – that is why I wanted to tell you – take care that you do not act wrongly tonight, more than ever in your life, so that our host cannot see anything that displeases him in you. Before he sits down to eat he will make you sit down first on a seat at the table, above everyone else and next to the most beautiful creature in the world – I mean his daughter. You and she will eat together. You can be sure that she will be sitting there. Your coming will be more welcome to her than that of any knight of her acquaintance. She knows your excellence and, it is said, has given away her heart out of her body. Once she explained it to me and said secretly, in confidence, that she would willingly be yours, would quietly and discreetly be yours in her room. But as she greatly fears her father, she will not wish for it to be noticed. Do not worry, I beg you, about the way that she will behave towards you, for God and for St Peter himself! I have stayed with her father more than thirty-one weeks; well I know how he carries on, and well I know him and his nature. Now you are certainly well informed and warned about it. You will be very foolish if you give yourself away to him, since it is essential that no-one should know anything about it. She will do enough to know your pleasure, but love makes many people foolish. She is mad for your love; so this is how she feels, and what her manner will be, and how the castle will appear.'

Sir Gawain said: 'Many thanks for telling me all this. I do not think that I shall do anything wrong, and if the lord has me taken prisoner, there will be no reason for his doing so.'

They said no more on this matter but rode on rapidly, and did not encounter any difficulty nor anything to annoy them, nor was their day tiresome. They had not rested their horses before they came to a lodging, after a time, at a castle close to some water. Neither my father nor my grandfather ever saw one so well situated, so that those within would never suffer because of an army encamped around it. On one side it had a very rich harbour, for on the water there were a great number of ships. I do not think that the revenue was smaller than that of Montpellier or of Pavia, because every day of the week they brought in five hundred and ten marks. The knights crossed the bridge and went through the great town and the market; but they did not stop to transact business, those barons, for they were not such people. They went to find their lodgings which were very well appointed, in the castle, below the tower. Every one of more than twenty knights, I believe, came to meet them, as well as the seneschal and the constables. The lord was playing at backgammon at the moment that they arrived, I understand. The two knights came together hand in hand to his table, and Hunbaut said:

'I bring you Gawain the nephew of the king as your guest.'

And he immediately rose from his game, jumping up to meet them straightaway, and said to Gawain:

'May God bless you; and welcome to my castle, since God has made you such that you have the highest reputation in all the world.'

Then he took him by the hand and made him disarm without

delay. There were enough there who knew how to wait on him, nor need anyone disbelieve me. Someone was sent into the best room where the clothes were kept for a robe which well suited him, and Sir Gawain sat down beside the lord on the left. So the lord enquired carefully how he was, how he was travelling and where he had come from. And Gawain, who well remembered and called to mind that he should always tell the truth, told him how the king had sent him so far away on his behalf. The lord was courteous and wise, and so did not speak of it further, but instead talked of something else; and he asked his servants if the food was ready, and who could tell him of something new. As soon as it suited the lord's pleasure the table was set up. The two knights climbed up into the hall by the stairs.

They graciously led in the girl who, in beauty and accomplishments, had no peer in the world – I am telling you the whole story here. Nature never knew how to make a better, as far as the arms or the body or the feet or the hands went, and all the rest had great beauty, too, by St. Herbert. She had fair hair which was uncovered, and a well-proportioned and graceful figure. The men were very eager to look at her with admiration. Sir Gawain marvelled at her: her beauty dazzled him, for it was not marred or flawed, she was so white and red together, the one colour blended with the other. But at length, to arrange the seating better, her father made her sit at the head of the others on the high table with all the most valiant in the world, and the man of whom I must tell you more, whom the lord took by the hand and seated beside his daughter. By every right he decided to seat Sir Gawain in this place, where he was looked at from more than one side as he talked to the girl. His heart counselled him as to what he should ask and require of her, and suggested that he could not seek a finer occasion to say to her what was appropriate, when no-one was sitting near them who could hear their words. I cannot think of any reason why he should have hung back, if the girl meant anything to him, for the father did not worry – on the contrary he was joyful and happy and merry. The host made Hunbaut, who was pleased with his welcome, eat with him. The girl behaved towards her guest Sir Gawain wisely and discreetly, and put aside embarrassment and disdain and anger, but she did not want to declare her full intentions. He gave very little thought to his replies, because he spoke to her first. He spoke of love in very beautiful words, and asked for her love. She did not hesitate all this time to reply to him immediately and always without contempt but simply with a pleasant manner, and she said:

'I shall value myself the more all the days of my life. I shall never, ever have any desire for love from any other but you. I have heard so much of your great fame, although I have never met you. And so I am very happy away from the crowd, to be beside you; but I am behaving more freely than ever I did before.'

Then they exchanged their faith and each gave assurances to the other. And so they talked together confidently there, each one looking long at the other. They did not think about whether anyone in the castle would be displeased or whether anyone sat eating opposite them at the table – there never was so much elegant and delightful talk heard at a meal before. They sat long at the meal, and yet they took very little of it. Gawain had learnt the nature and the custom of the castle for nothing: of her alone had he any awareness. Hunbaut, who had put him to school, loved him almost better than Nicole and the girl together, but their behaviour seemed incorrect. So he looked frequently in their direction, overcome with fear and anxiety, so that all his limbs shook. He could not make Gawain call his warning to mind, nor her who sat next to him, because of one thought which possessed their minds – of no other were they conscious. And they were so absorbed with what had happened to them there, that they could not withdraw their hearts. The servants had the cloths removed when the occasion and the moment and the hour had come; the water was brought to them in bowls of silver, and the towel was quite ready. Each one hurried about his business so that he was not blamed for bad service. Clear and sparkling wine in costly cups was brought in again, and the knights went away after a long while to many different places.

When the time to sleep was near the girl went away. The lord left his place and came into the room, stopping by the door. Then he took her by her white hand and said:

'You must be very badly brought up, to have taken such brief leave of the wisest and most accomplished man that one could find anywhere, the one that you have just left. You and he ate together, so you will kiss, as it seems good to me to do so, just once, as you take your leave.'

Gawain did not think of doing anything wrong, but four times and without shyness, he gladly went to kiss her: he had not thought that he would have such good fortune.

'By all the saints that one has ever heard of' said the rich man, who was very angry, 'now that is too much from this lord, who has taken no notice of my words. By my reckoning he has kissed my daughter three times more than I said. Now he values my words too little, but he will find out what I mean to do. Get both his eyes put out and then he can be thrown into my prison. He has committed too great an offence, so he certainly ought to come to grief. When Arthur wants to come here to retaliate, let him come! I don't expect to have to arm myself for fear of all his troops. Let him come to me, if he has the strength! His power is scarcely worth anything.'

Then Sir Gawain was taken away and ill-treated, as I have heard, but all the knights said to their lord together:

'That is ill done! You have committed many outrages, but nothing as bad as this. Not one of us will ever attempt to make his escape in any direction, to prevent our souls being separated from our bodies by burning or hanging. Hunbaut never came here to give away the eyes of the king's nephew. It would be considered a great offence if he paid so dear a tax. There is not a Cornishman or a Scotsman in this country that would not repudiate such a deed rather than carry it out, because it is neither reasonable nor right.'

Immediately, the lord acquiesced, as soon as he heard the grounds on which those who gave him loyal advice advocated restraint. And in the hearing of all, and in council there, they said a good deal to the effect that Sir Gawain behaved correctly to the great man, in their view:

'Another time, beware of wrong-doing if you wish to be wise.'

The valets ran to make the beds, when this deed had been pardoned. She who had given her love utterly to Sir Gawain was very angry that he was so soon going away from her father's castle, but she was very careful that it should not be noticed, and meanwhile, when it grew dark, she came in the night to lie beside Sir Gawain, not bringing to his bedside maidens or ladies in great numbers.

'Indeed, if I did not love you very much,' she said as she lay down with him, 'I would never lie in this bed, for I take on me a great burden.'

And she took him between her arms and so they lay all that night together. - Badly watched means you have it stolen. - And when morning came, so that she did not dare to stay longer, she said goodbye when dawn broke. She began to weep bitterly, as she said goodbye with sweet kisses. They did not know how to tell each other that it was the end of their time together. Very quietly and secretly the girl went away. And so this thing came about, which stirred her heart and caused it to be uplifted. And Sir Gawain got up, he and Hunbaut, when it was day, for they had no desire to stay longer – they had many other affairs in hand. They had said goodbye the evening before; in their anxiety to get up in the morning they had no thought of staying and so they quickly dressed themselves and then they left the castle.

From *Hunbaut*, ed. J. Sturzinger and H. Breuer, Dresden 1914, lines 49–846.

The Knight of the Sword

Those who love amusement and delight, come forward and listen, and hear a tale of an adventure which befell a noble knight who upheld loyalty, prowess and honour, and who never loved, ever, cowardly, false or base men. I shall tell you about Sir Gawain who was so very well-bred and so highly esteemed for his fighting that no-one could adequately describe him. Anyone who wanted to give an account of all his good qualities and set them down briefly would never come to the end of them. If I cannot tell you all of them, I ought not on that account to be silent, however, and not relate them at all. In my opinion, one ought not to blame Chrétien, who knew how to tell about King Arthur, and about his court and his company, who were so much praised and admired. Chrétien also made stories about the deeds of the others and yet never told a story about Gawain, much too worthy a man to be forgotten. And so it gives me pleasure to tell for the first time of an adventure which happened to the good knight.

One summer King Arthur was at his city of Carlisle. With him were the queen and Gawain, but of the others, only Kay the Seneschal and Yvain came too. Every day Gawain indulged his inclination to go and amuse and enjoy himself. When he had made ready his horse, he equipped himself elegantly. He put on a pair of spurs made of gold over his cut-away hose of well-embroidered silken cloth. He put on breeches, very white and very fine, a shortish, wide shirt of linen finely pleated, and donned his fur-lined cloak. He was very richly dressed. Then he went out of the town. He took the way which went to the right, so that he entered the forest. He listened to the song of the birds, which were singing very sweetly. For a long time he listened to them, for he heard a great many of them, and so he fell into a reverie about an adventure that he called to mind that had happened to him. So long he lingered there that he went astray in the forest and so lost his way. The sun went down as he began to muse; and evening was coming on when he came out of his reverie. He had no idea where he was, and so he thought that he would turn back. Then he came to a cart-track which continually went on before him; and it grew still darker, so that he did not know where to go. He began to look intently before him down the track through a clearing, and there he saw a great fire lighted. He went slowly in that direction because he thought that he might find a man who would put him on his way, a wood-cutter or a charcoal-burner. Then he saw near the fire a warhorse, which was tied up to a tree. He went over to the fire and there he saw a knight sitting. He greeted him at once:

'May that God who has made the world and placed the souls in our bodies,' he said, 'grant you, good sir, a large share in Him.'

'Friend,' replied the knight, 'may God protect you, too. Tell me whence you have come, you who go alone at such an hour.'

And Gawain told him the whole truth from beginning to end: how he went out to enjoy himself, and then how he got lost in the forest because of his day-dream, in which he so completely forgot everything that he lost his way. And the knight undertook to put him back on his way in the morning with a good will, provided only that he would stay and bear him company until the night was past. This request was granted. He laid down his lance and shield, dismounted from his horse and tied it to a small tree, covered himself with his cloak and then sat down beside the fire. The knight asked him how he had travelled that day, and Gawain told him everything – he never deigned to lie to him. However, the knight acted treacherously; never a word of truth did he speak to him – you will hear in full why he did it. When they had watched long enough and talked of many things, they fell asleep by the fire. At daybreak Sir Gawain woke first, and then the other knight.

'My house is very close to here – two leagues away and no more – and so I beg you to come to it. You may be sure of very fine lodging there, and welcome to it,' he said.

Then they mounted their warhorses, took their shields, their lances and their swords and set out at once on a metalled road. They had not gone very far before they were out of the forest and in the open countryside. Then the knight spoke to Gawain:

'Sir,' he said, 'listen to this. It is always the custom and indeed the accepted thing, when a courteous and worthy knight brings another with him, that he should go ahead of him to make his lodging ready, so that he will find everything at hand, and so that on his arrival he will not find anything which might displease him. I have no-one to send, as you can clearly see, apart from myself. So I beg you, if it is not displeasing to you, to come along at your own pace, and I will go ahead with all haste. You will see my house beside an enclosure straight ahead, in a valley.'

Gawain knew well that what he said was right and proper, and so he went at a slow pace while the other went on with great speed. On this direct route, Sir Gawain came upon four shepherds who had stopped beside the track. They greeted him courteously, and he returned their greeting in the name of God, went past them, and said no more.

'Ah, what a misfortune' said one of them, 'for such a noble, handsome, elegant knight! Indeed, it is a great shame that he should be wounded or injured.'

Gawain, when he had heard these words, was completely amazed. He immediately began to wonder greatly to himself why they lamented for him when they did not know him at all. Quickly he returned to them and greeted them all once again, then courteously asked them to tell him the truth about why they had said that he was unlucky. One of them answered him:

'Sir,' said he, 'we are sorry because we see that you are following the knight who went ahead on an iron-grey horse. Before our very eyes he has led many off, but we have never yet seen any who have ever returned.'

And Gawain said:

'Friend, do you know if he did any good to them or not?'

'Sir, it is said in this countryside that the man who gainsays him in anything, whatever it is, either bad or good, he kills in his own house. We only know what we have heard tell, for nobody ever saw anyone who has returned from there; and if you will believe us, do not follow him a foot further forward if you value your life. You are an extremely handsome knight, and it would be a pity if he killed you.'

And Sir Gawain said to them:

'Shepherds, I commend you to God. I do not intend to abandon my route through his territory for a child's tale.'

If it became known in his country that he had hesitated for such a thing, he would have been reproached to the end of his days. He journeyed on with his horse at a walking pace, thinking of this, until he came to the valley which the other knight had pointed out to him. Beside a great enclosure, surmounting a mound, he saw a fine castle which had recently been fortified. He saw a wide, deep ditch, and the bailey in front of the bridge had very fine outbuildings. Never in his life had Gawain ever seen anything richer belonging either to a prince or a king. But I do not wish to stop to describe the outbuildings, except to say that they were very fine and costly. He came up to the tilting-ground but then went in through the gate and crossed the courtyard and came to the end of the bridge. The lord hurried up to meet him, making a great appearance of being delighted at his coming. A squire received his weapons, another took Gringalet, a third removed his spurs. Then his host took him by the hand and led him over the bridge, and they found a very fine fire in the room facing the tower, and a very rich seat covered with silken fabric all round. They stabled his horse on one side (in such a way that he could see it) and someone brought it plenty of fodder and hay. Gawain thanked them for everything, and in nothing did they wish to oppose his wishes. The host said to him:

'Good sir, your dinner is being prepared, and I can assure you that the servants are hurrying as much as they can to get it ready for you. Now if meanwhile you will amuse yourself, you can be quite free and at your ease. If there is anything that displeases you, say so without hesitation.'

Gawain said that the lodging was arranged entirely according to his liking. The lord went into one of the rooms to look for his daughter – there was no girl in all the land who came anywhere near her for excellence. I could not describe in a day all the beauty or even half of it with which she was filled and adorned, nor do I wish to pass it over, so I will describe it in a few words. Everything that nature knew how to devise that might be pleasing in a human body in the way of grace and of beauty was united in her. The host, who was no peasant, took her by the right hand and led her to the hall. And Gawain when he had gazed on her great beauty, was very nearly overwhelmed, yet nevertheless he jumped up. The girl, even more, when she had looked at Gawain, was overwhelmed by his good looks and by his noble bearing. And meanwhile, courteously and in brief words he greeted her. At once the host presented her by the hand to Sir Gawain, and he said to him:

'I bring you my daughter, if it does not displease you, for I have no more splendid entertainment to charm and please you. She well knows how to keep you excellent company if she wishes. It is my wish that she should not refuse. There is so much feeling and spirit in you that if she were to fall in love with you, she would find in it nothing but honour. As for me, I give you this assurance, that I will never be grudging towards you; on the contrary, I command her in your hearing that she shall never oppose you in anything.'

Gawain thanked him politely, not wishing to gainsay him; and the other went out forthwith towards the kitchen to ask if it was possible to dine fairly soon. Gawain sat down beside the girl, very worried because of his host, whom he greatly feared, but nevertheless he immediately spoke courteously and without a trace of impoliteness to the girl with the fair hair. He spoke neither too much nor too little, talked discreetly with her, and very handsomely offered her his service, and spoke so much of his feelings that she, who was sensible and wise, understood and fully realised that he would love her above all else if it should be to her pleasure. Then she did not know what to do, whether to refuse or to accept him: he had spoken so courteously to her and she had seen such good manners in him that she would have quite fallen in love with him, had she dared to reveal it; but on no account would she consent to make her feelings known to him when he could not carry it any further. She well knew that she would be acting in an uncourtly way if she caused him to suffer from love-sickness from which he could never recover completely; but to refuse him was difficult for her, so much was her heart drawn towards him. Then she spoke courteously to him:

'Sir,' she said, 'I understand that my father has forbidden me to oppose you in anything. Now I only know that I must tell you that, if I do consent to fulfil your wish I shall never bring it to a successful conclusion. Instead, I shall have betrayed and killed you. But of one thing I warn you, and in good faith I say it to you, that you beware of base conduct; in nothing that my father says to you, whatever it may be, whether good or bad, can you oppose him in the slightest without peril, for if you do, you will be dead on the spot. You would be ill-advised even to give a hint of being aware of anything.'

And now the host, who had gone to the kitchen, returned and the food was ready, and the water called for; he had no wish to wait any longer. When they had washed they sat down and the servants laid the overcloths on top of the white and beautiful tablecloths, the dishes and the knives, then the bread, and then the wine and cups of silver and fine gold. But I do not wish to stop longer, to specify the dishes one by one; for they had plenty of meat and fish, roast birds and venison, and joyfully they ate their fill, and the host absolutely insisted that Gawain and the girl should drink, and so he said to the girl that she should urge the knight. And he said:

'You should deeply appreciate that I intend her to love you.'

Gawain thanked him politely.

When they had eaten enough the servants were in readiness, and they removed the tablecloths and the overcloths, and they brought them water and the towel to dry on. After the meal the host said that he wished to go to see his woods and so he asked Gawain to sit and amuse himself with the lady, at the same time calling him aside to tell him not to go away before he came back; and he instructed a servant that if he appeared to want anything, he should provide it immediately. Gawain, who was noble and courteous, saw clearly that he must remain and that he could not do otherwise, so he said immediately that he had no desire to go, since he wished to stay there. The host mounted his horse and went off at top speed. He went to seek another adventure, for he was certain of this one that he had enclosed within his walls. The girl took Gawain by the hand, and they sat on one side so as to discuss how he could protect himself. Sweetly and charmingly she comforted him, but she was worried to death about it, because she knew the idea that her father had in mind. If she knew how, she would have shown him by what device he could escape, but her father never wished her to say anything about it. But she took care not to oppose him, so that Gawain could by some means escape.

'Now let us stay here,' he said. 'It will do me no harm. He brought me to his house and has given me a very warm welcome. Since he has done me honour and good, never from now onwards will I fear anything at all unless I should discover or perceive any reason for which I ought to fear him.'

She said to him:

'It is of no use. There used to be a common saying, and many people do still say, that you should only praise the day in the evening when you see that it has ended well, and the same about one's host in the morning. And may God, in accordance with my desire, grant that you may leave your host in joy and without ill-will.'

When they had talked for a long time and spoken much of this and that, the host returned to his castle. Gawain sprang up to welcome him, with the girl, hand in hand; they greeted him very sweetly. He told them that he was in a great hurry because he was afraid that if he had lingered, Gawain would have gone away already, not wishing to remain longer. It began to get dark and the host asked the servants what there was for supper. His daughter said to him:

'At your pleasure you can ask for wine and fruit, but nothing else by right. You have eaten enough already.'

He then ordered it. They first washed, and then the fruit was set before him, and the servants brought wine, in plenty, of every kind.

'Sir, take your pleasure,' he said to Sir Gawain. 'Of one thing you may be certain: it grieves me and often distresses me when I give hospitality to some one who does not enjoy it and who does not express his desires.'

'Know the truth, sir,' said Gawain: 'I am entirely contented.'

When they had eaten the fruit the host ordered the beds to be made and said:

'I will lie down in this room, and this knight in my bed; do not make it too small, because my daughter will lie with him. With so good a knight I think that she will be well occupied. She should be very happy at what he has promised her.'

Both of them thanked him for it and pretended that it pleased them very much. Gawain was now very anxious because he believed that if he went to bed the host would have him cut in pieces, and he also realised that if he refused, he would kill him in his castle.

The host hurried to go to bed; he took Gawain by the hand and led him into the room immediately. The girl with the fresh face went with him too. The room was well adorned with tapestries and twelve candles were burning there, completely encircling the bed and giving forth a very great brightness. The bed, too, was well adorned with rich quilts and white sheets – but I do not wish to linger in describing the richness of the silken hangings from Palermo and Rome with which the room was decorated, or the sables, the light-coloured and the grey furs. To put it in a single word: whatever was appropriate for a knight, or to adorn the person of a lady both in winter and in summer, was there in very great quantity – it had very rich furnishings. Gawain was very much astonished at the richness that he saw, and the knight said to him:

'Sir, this room is very beautiful. Both you and this girl shall lie here, and nobody else. Shut the doors, my girl, and do what he tells you, for I know very well that such nobles have no need of a crowd. But this much I want to warn you: do not extinguish the candles or I shall be very angry. I wish, since I have commanded it, that he may see your great beauty when you lie in his arms, so that he shall have greater pleasure and so that you may see his handsome body.'

Then he withdrew from the room and the girl shut the doors. Sir Gawain lay down, and she returned to the bed and lay down beside him naked – no request was necessary. And she lay all night long between his arms, very sweetly. He kissed and hugged her often, and in fact had gone so far that he would soon have accomplished his desire when she said:

'Sir, enough! Things must not go on like this. I am not without consideration for you.'

Gawain looked all round but he could not see a living thing there.

'Darling,' he said, 'I want to know what it is that you say prevents me from having my desire of you.'

She replied:.

'I will most willingly tell you what I know about it. Do you see this sword which hangs here, which has this silver ornamentation, and a pommel and hilt of fine gold? I am not guessing about this thing that you will hear me tell you of now; rather, I have seen it well tried out. My father is very fond of this device, with which he has frequently killed very good and valued knights. Believe me, in here alone, he has killed more than twenty of them; but I do not know whence it came to them. Never shall there enter through this door a knight who shall escape alive. My father makes them very welcome, but if he catches one in the smallest fault he kills him. One must beware of base deeds; well it becomes one to act aright. He immediately inflicts justice on him if he can catch him out in the slightest thing. And if a man takes such good care that he is not caught out in anything, he is made to spend the night with me. Then he meets his death; do you know why there is no escape? If he appears in any way to fulfill with me the desire by which he is seized, at once the sword strikes him on his body. And if he tries to go and grasp it and to snatch it away, it immediately jumps out of its sheath at him and strikes him on the body. So you realise that the sword which guards me all the time in this way is indeed in some way enchanted. Now you should be forewarned by me, for you are so courteous and wise that it would be a very great pity and it would grieve me ever afterwards if you were killed for me.'

Now Gawain did not know what to do. Never before in the whole of his life had he ever heard tell of such a dire threat, and so he suspected that she had told him all this to protect herself, so that he could not satisfy his desire. On the other hand, he reflected, it could not be concealed – indeed would be generally known – that he had lain with her all alone, both of them naked, in her bed, and that he had, on account of a single word, desisted from making love to her. It is more becoming to die in honour than to live long in shame.

'Darling,' he said, 'that's nothing. Since I am here, I just want to be your lover. You can't avoid it.'

'You can't blame me for it from now on,' she said.

He came so close to her that she cried out, and the sword leapt from the sheath and dealt him a glancing blow on the side so that he was struck on the skin but not severely wounded. It pierced through the quilt and through all the sheets as far as the mattress, then went back into its scabbard. Gawain was left completely amazed and quite lost all his desire, as he lay beside her utterly taken aback.

'Sir,' she said, 'for God's sake, enough! You think that I told you because I wanted to defend myself from you in this situation, but in fact I have never told any knight about this but you. And you can be sure that it is a great wonder that you are not utterly dead on the spot from the first blow. For God's sake now, do lie down in peace and take care from now on not to touch me in any way. A wise man may inadvertently undertake something which turns out to his disadvantage.'

Gawain remained dejected and cast down because he did not know how to behave. If God granted that he should return to his own land again, this affair could never be concealed, and it would be known everywhere that he had lain all alone at night with such a beautiful and charming girl, and yet had never done anything to her. And she had not opposed him with anything more than the threat of a sword wielded by nobody! So now he would be shamed all his days, if she eluded him thus. And so the candles that he saw around him which gave a very bright light caused him very great irritation, for by them he saw her great beauty. Her hair was blonde, her forehead broad and her eyebrows delicate; her eyes were sparkling, her nose well shaped and her complexion fresh and bright, with a small and laughing mouth. Her neck was long and graceful, her hands white and her sides soft and curved – under the sheets her body was white and tender. No-one could have found any fault in her, she had so graceful and well-made a figure. He drew close to her very gently because he was not a peasant. He was playing a certain game when the sword jumped from its scabbard and made another attack on him; the flat struck him on the neck. He very nearly took himself for a fool. But the sword was deflected a little and turned to his right shoulder so that it cut three fingers' breadths in the skin and caused a piece to be cut out of the silken quilt. Then it thrust itself back into its sheath. When Gawain felt himself wounded in the shoulder and on the side, and saw that he could not achieve success, he was much grieved and did not know what to do, and he was very exasperated at his situation.

'Sir,' she said 'are you dead?'

' Lady,' he replied, 'I am not; but for the rest of this night I give you this assurance, that you shall have a truce with me.'

'Sir,' said she, 'by my faith, if it had been given when it was asked for it would now be much pleasanter for you.'

Gawain was much anguished by this, and the girl as well. Neither the one nor the other slept, but watched in great grief all night long until morning. Prompt and early the host got up when it was day, and came into the bedroom. He was far from being silent or dumb, but called very loudly, and the girl immediately opened the door and then came back, so she was beside Gawain lying naked. And the knight came in after. He saw them both lying in peace, and asked them how they were, and Sir Gawain replied:

'Very well, thank you, sir.'

When the knight heard that he spoke so clearly, you may guess that he was most upset, since he was wicked and ill-natured.

'What!' he said, 'Are you alive?'

'Indeed,' said Sir Gawain, 'I am perfectly well and healthy. I assure you that I have not done anything for which I ought to be done to death, and if in your own house, without a reason, you do me evil and harm, it would be very wrong.'

'What!' said he, 'So you are not dead? It much annoys me that you are alive.'

Then he came forward a little, so that he plainly saw the quilt which had been cut and the blood-stained bed-linen.

'Fellow,' he said, 'now tell me straightaway where this blood comes from.'

And Sir Gawain paused, because he did not want to lie to him, and because he knew no explanation under which he could well shield himself, that the host would not see through. The host soon spoke:

'Fellow,' he said, 'listen here. You can conceal nothing from me. You wished to have your desire of this girl, but you could not succeed because of the sword which prevented it.'

And Sir Gawain said to him:

'Sir, you speak truth: the sword has wounded me in two places, but has not injured me severely.'

And when the knight heard that he was not mortally wounded, he said:

'You have come to a good place, good sir. But now if you want to get off completely, tell me your country and your name, of what family, of what reputation and of what rank you are, so that all your wishes may be fulfilled. I want to be quite certain.'

'Sir,' he said, 'I am called Gawain and I am the nephew of good King Arthur. You can be sure of this, that I have never changed my name.'

'Indeed,' said the host, 'I know very well, that in you he has a very good knight. I find none better spoken of. Neither in your land as far as Majorca, nor in all the kingdom of Logres could a better be found. I will tell you how I have proved it. All the knights in the world who go to seek adventures, could they have lain in this bed, would all have had to die one after the other, until it chanced that the very best should come. The sword would choose him for me, because it would not kill the best knight when he came. And now one has truly stood the test, for the sword has chosen you as the best; and when God bestows honour on you, I do not know how to choose or to find one who would be worthier to have my daughter. I grant her to you and bestow her on you. No evil whatsoever from now on need you fear from me. And so I give you the command of this castle, in good faith, for all the days of your life; do with it what you will.'

Then Gawain, who was overjoyed and delighted at this, thanked him for it.

'Sir,' said he, 'I am well rewarded with the girl alone; I have no desire for your gold or for your silver, nor for this castle.'

Then both Gawain and the girl got up, as was fitting.

All through the region went the news that a knight was come who wished to have the girl – a knight on whom the sword had been twice drawn, but without doing any harm to him. And they all vied with each other to be the first to come. There was very great joy in the castle among the ladies and the knights, and very rich was the feast that the father had prepared. But I do not want to stop to tell what the dishes were, for they ate and drank a great deal. When they had eaten their fill and the cloths were removed, the entertainers of whom there were many, each showed what he could do. One tuned his viol, another fluted, another played the reed-pipes, and the others sang part-songs and played either on the harp or on the rote; some read tales and some told stories. Some knights played backgammon, or on the other hand, chess or dice or games of chance. They spent their time thus all the day until nightfall and then they supped with great delight; there were birds in plenty and fruit, and a great deal of good wine. When they had happily finished their supper, they very soon went to bed. They immediately conducted the girl and Sir Gawain to the room where they had lain the night before, and the host went with them, and married them with good will, and joined together the girl and the knight without further obstacle. He then came out and shut the door. What more would you have me tell you? That night he had his desire, and no sword was unsheathed there. If he returned again to the attack on the courteous damsel, it does not distress me, and she was not upset.

So Gawain remained a long time in the castle with great joy and delight. When he thought to himself that he had stayed there a long time, so that his relations and friends would certainly think that he had been killed, he went to the host to ask for leave to go:

'Sir,' he said, 'I have stayed a very long time in this land, so that my friends and family must think that I am lost. And so I ask for leave to go away, of your grace, and that you will see that this lady is adorned in such a way that I may have honour in taking her, and you in giving her to me; and so that when I come into my own country it may be said that I have a beautiful beloved and that she is come from a good family.'

The host gave him leave and Gawain went back to his own country and the girl with him. The palfrey on which the girl was mounted was richly adorned at bridle and saddle; Gawain was mounted on his horse. Why should I make you a longer tale of it?

He took the arms that he had brought and with the leave of the host he went away, happy and rejoicing in the adventure.

[Here a line is missing in the original.]

And when she came outside the gate the girl drew rein. He asked her what it meant.

'Sir,' said she, 'I have an obligation that I have allowed to be completely forgotten. You may be sure that I shall leave this country very unwillingly without my greyhounds that I have reared myself, which are very fine and well-bred. You never saw swifter ones, and they are whiter than any flower.'

Then Gawain turned back again and went for the greyhounds at a gallop, and the host who had clearly seen him coming a long way off, went to meet him.

'Gawain,' he said, 'for what need have you returned so soon?'

'Sir,' said he, 'because your daughter has forgotten her greyhounds, and she tells me that they are very dear to her and that she will not go on without them.'

And the host called them and handed them over very willingly, and Gawain returned very promptly with all the greyhounds to the girl who was waiting for him. Then they resumed their journey and entered the forest by the way they had come. Then they saw a knight who was coming towards them along the way. The knight came all alone but he was completely armed so that he lacked nothing of whatever is needful for a knight, and he was mounted on a bay horse, strong and swift and lively. The knight came on apace until he was quite close to them, and Gawain intended to greet him in peace and then to enquire who he was and of what land. But the other, who had different ideas, spurred his horse so sharply that it leapt forward – and never a word was heard – between the girl and Gawain, and he took her by the bridle and at once turned back again, and she, without any further request, went immediately to him. If Gawain was angry and disgusted when he saw the knight lead her off like that, he did not resist because he bore no arms except for shield and lance and sword, and the other who was very well armed was strong and huge and proud, so that Gawain was at a disadvantage compared with him. So Gawain did not contend with him on horseback for the girl like a bold man.

'Knight,' he said, 'you have performed a very base deed in so harshly seizing my beloved, but now do a bold action in the way I shall devise. You can clearly see that I have nothing except for my lance and my shield and the sword hanging at my side. I call upon you to disarm so that we may be on an equal footing, and you will do me a very great courtesy. And if you can win her from me by chivalry, she shall be yours without further fighting. And if you do not wish to do this, be courteous and honourable and wait for me on my undertaking. I shall go and borrow some arms from one of my friends nearby and when I am equipped with armour I will return at once. And then if you can win her from me, I will hand her over to you without resentment. So, truly, I promise you.'

And he replied at once:

'You will never have leave to go. And because I have not acted wrongly at all I shall never ask pardon of you. If you make me a present of what is my own, you certainly are very powerful. Since you are unarmed, and so that you need not continue in wrong-doing, there is already a choice open to you. You say that she is your beloved because she has come with you, and I say on my part that she is mine; now put her in the road and each of us can go to one side. Then it is entirely up to her to decide which she loves most: and if she wishes to go to you, I consent and hand her over to you; if she wishes to come to me, it is therefore right that she should be mine.'

Gawain willingly granted him this, for he trusted and loved her so much that he was certain that he would find that she would not leave him for the world. So they left her, and they went off, each withdrawing a little to one side.

'Darling,' they said, 'now there is nothing more. It is all a matter of your pleasure, as to which one you wish to stay with, because that is what we have agreed.'

She looked from one to the other, first at him and then at Gawain, who really thought that he was quite sure and absolutely certain to have her; and he wondered to himself what she was thinking. But the girl, who knew very well how Gawain could acquit himself in love, wanted next to know about the knight, and how bold and valiant he was. You all, both great and small, and those who laugh as well as those who groan, know that there is scarcely a woman in the world, if she is a sweetheart and a wife, with the best knight there can be from here to Greater India, who would ever love him enough to value him as much as a pinch of salt if he was not valiant in the castle – you all know to what prowess I refer. Now listen to this most deplorable deed that this young woman did: in the look she gave him she implied that she did not know him in the slightest, and when Sir Gawain saw it you may be sure that he was most indignant that she had thrown him over of her own free will. But he was both brave and clever, and so courteous and so intelligent that never a word did he speak to her although he was most upset. And the knight said to him:

'Sir,' he said, 'without a doubt the girl must belong to me.'

'May God never look upon me,' said Gawain, 'if I offer any opposition, or ever fight for a thing for which I have no desire.'

So then the girl and the knight went off in a great hurry, and Gawain, with all the greyhounds, went off towards his own land. As soon as she was at the very end of the open country the girl stopped and the knight asked her why she had stopped.

'Sir,' said she, 'I shall never be your beloved for so much as a day until I am in possession of my greyhounds that I see that that fellow is leading away with him.'

And he said to her:

'You shall have them.'

Then he cried, 'Stop! stop! You fellow, I command you that you go no further forward.'

Then they very quickly came up with him.

'Fellow,' said he, 'why do you carry off the greyhounds when they are not yours?'

And Sir Gawain replied:

'Sir,' he said, 'I keep them for mine, and if no-one else claims them, I shall keep them as my own. And if you want to take them, I will willingly permit you the choice that you offered me when you set the girl in the middle of the road for her to choose with whom she wished to stay.'

And the knight willingly agreed to accept the choice, for like a wicked man he thought that if the greyhounds would come to him without a fight, they would remain with him; and he could also be quite certain that if they went over to Gawain he would be able to carry them off immediately in the same way as he would now do. Then they left them in the road. When they were at a distance they each called them and the greyhounds went straight to Gawain whom they recognised because they had seen him so much alone at the girl's father's. Gawain caressed them and called them because he was very happy to have them. And there and then the girl addressed the knight:

'Sir,' she said, 'never a single step will I go with you in the sight of God until I am in possession of my greyhounds that I love so much.'

And he replied,

'Without my consent he cannot take them away.'

Then he said:

'Fellow, let them be. You will never take them away.'

And Gawain said:

'If you go back on your word in this way it will be a disgraceful action; but I am in possession of the greyhounds, as they came to me of their own free will. May God in His majesty never help me when I fail them. I gave the girl up to you merely because she clung to you, even though she was mine and came with me; and therefore you ought without hesitation to allow the greyhounds to remain with me, as is right, since they are mine and came with me, and stay with me of their own free will. One thing you can be sure of, and you can see it by me, if you hope to satisfy the demands of this girl you will have little joy of her – I hope she can hear what I'm saying – for I can assure you that when she was mine she got what she wanted, and now see how she has served me! It doesn't happen like that with this dog as it does with the woman, as you can see: he will never change the master who has reared him for a stranger. A woman completely throws over her master if he does not give her all she wants, and it is an astonishing thing about such an exchange that she will leave her own for a stranger. The hounds have not deserted me by which I can easily prove – and it will never be contradicted in any way – that the nature and the love of the dog is better than anything that women can offer.'

'Fellow,' he replied, 'your argument does you no good here. If you do not immediately yield, watch out, for I defy you.'

Then Gawain seized his shield and pulled it in front of his breast, and then each charged the other as fast as his horse could gallop. Then the knight struck him with such violence right on the boss of the shield that he broke it to pieces, and smashed it so that the splinters flew from it as far and high as the flight of an arrow. And after that Gawain struck him on the first quarter of the shield so hard, as I understand, that he and his horse together fell in a rut. He fell into a muddy pool, still astride his horse. And

Gawain drew his sword of steel the moment he turned, and as soon as he could dismount he attacked him on the ground. He struck him a great blow in the face and on the head, so that he was quite stunned. He exerted all his strength, for he hated him greatly because of the wrong he had done him and because of the vexation he had caused him. Much he injured him and much he wounded him; he lifted up the edge of his hauberk and then thrust his good sword into his side. Then he left him when he was avenged. He did not wish ever to see again either horse, or hauberk or shield. So he went to call the greyhounds that he had so much loved, and which had so well shown their worth to him. And then he ran to catch his horse which had strayed off into the woods. Quickly he caught him and took him. He never needed stirrups to jump into the saddle.

'Sir,' said the girl to him, 'for God's sake and for your honour I beg you that you will not leave me here. That would be a very dastardly deed. If I was foolish and stupid you ought not to make me suffer for it. I did not dare to go with you, because I was so frightened when I saw that you were so poorly equipped with arms, and he was armed so very well that he lacked for nothing.'

'My lovely girl,' he said, 'that won't do. Your tricks won't help you, and this deceit is quite useless. Such faith, such love, such a nature one can often find in a woman. Whoever expects to reap from his field a different crop from what he has sown, and whoever hopes to find in a woman what is not in her nature, is not wise. Things have always been like this since God made the first woman. The more you take trouble to serve them, and the more you work for their advantage and honour, the more you regret it in the end; and the more you honour and serve them, the more you are vexed and the more you lose. Your consideration for me never came to you from concern for my honour and my life, but it came to you from a different source. It is a common saying that 'In the end, everything reveals its true nature.' Henceforth, may God never have in his protection the man who finds a woman deceitful and false and still cherishes her and loves her and keeps her. Now look after yourself.'

Thereupon he left her on her own, so that he had no idea of what became of her. He returned to his proper road and thought deeply about his adventure. He travelled so long through the forest that in the evening he came to his own land. His friends were overjoyed – they thought that they had lost him. He told

them of his adventure, just as it was, from beginning to end –
very willingly did they listen to it – his adventure at first
delightful and dangerous, and later unpleasant and troublesome,
because of his mistress whom he had lost, and then how he
fought for the greyhounds at great risk to himself.

And so it is all brought to an end.

Le Chevalier à L'Epée ed. E.C. Armstrong, Baltimore 1900.
(See also *Two Old French Gauvain Romances*, ed. R.C. Johnston and
D.D.R. Owen, Scottish Academic Press 1972. Texts of *Le Chevalier à
l'Epée* and *La Mule Sans Frein* with Introduction, Notes and Glossary,
and Parallel Readings with *Sir Gawain and the Green Knight*.)

EIGHT

The Antifeminist Diatribe

Sir Bors answers the queen's denunciation of Sir Lancelot

'My Lady,' said Bors, 'what can I say? I have certainly never seen any noble man that loved a woman for a long time, who was not finally held to be dishonoured, and if you reflect on the ancient deeds of the Jews and Saracens, you could learn about many who history affirms were dishonoured by a woman. Consider the story of King David: you will read that he had a son, the most beautiful creature that ever God made, who waged war against his father under the instigation of a woman, and died a shameful death. So you can see that the most handsome of the Jews died because of a woman. Then you can see in the same story that Solomon to whom God gave wisdom beyond the comprehension of a mortal mind, and also knowledge, denied God for a woman and was dishonoured and deceived. Samson, who was the strongest man in the world, died through a woman. Noble Hector and Achilles, who in arms and chivalry surpassed all other knights in ancient times, were both killed, and more than a hundred thousand with them, all because of one woman whom Paris took by force in Greece. In our time too, it is less than five years since the death of Tristan, the nephew of King Mark, who loved fair Yseut so faithfully that he never did anything to harm her in all his life. What more can I say? No man ever became deeply involved in love who did not die as a result'.

From *The Death of King Arthur* (*La Mort le Roi Artu*) translated by James Cable, Penguin, 1971, pp. 77–8.

From Kyng Alisaunder

Adam was byswike[1] of Eve;
And Sampson theo fort, also,
Daliada dude him wrong and wo;
And Davyd the kyng was brought of lyf
Thorugh the gyle of his wyf;
And Salamon, for a womanis love,
Forsok his God that syt above.

Kyng Alisaunder, ed. cit. lines 7709–15.

From Lydgate's Fall of Princes

Some princes justify their licentiousness by reference to biblical precedent: e.g.

Bexaumple off David, which that took Bersabe,
And for hir sake how he slouh Urie,
Dede manslauhtre and fals avoutrie, –
For hem aleggyng, ageyn riht and resoun,
For Dalida the luxure[2] off Sampsoun.

The stori also thei frowardli applie,
How for a woman prudent Salamoun,
The Lord offendyng, dede ydolatrie.
And in diffence off ther opynyoun,
Reherse these storyes for excusacioun
Off ther errour, therbi a pris to wynne,
As tofor God lecheri wer no synne.

Thei nat considre in ther entencioun
Off these stories everi circumstance:
First off kyng David the gret contricioun,
Nor upon Sampson how God took gret vengaunce;
First how he loste his force and his puissaunce
For his offence – thei have nat this in mynde,
Nor how that bothe his eien wer maad blynde.

Nor ther resouns thei list nat to enclyne
For to conceyve in their discrecioun,

---

[1] betrayed
[2] lust

The sperit off wisdam, hevenli and dyvyne,
Was take away for prudent Salamoun
In chastisyng for his transgressioun.
And summe doctours affermen overmore,
How Salamon repentid hym ful sore.

From *Lydgate's Fall of Princes*, ed. Henry Bergen, Part II (Books III–V),
Washington 1923, Book III, lines 1172–97.

Another warning to princes against dissolute habits

The chose off God, David the worthi kyng,
Prophete off prophetis, most sovereyn off renoun,
On Bersabe for a sodeyn lokyng
To slen Urie cauhte occasioun.
For which he suffred gret punycioun,
Chastised off God, he and al his hous,
For cause onli that he was lecherous.

Gret repentaunce he hadde and gret sorwyng,
And made psalmis off gret contricioun,
With woful teris and manyfold wepyng
To make a-seeth[1] for his transgressioun,
Yevyng to pryncis ful cleer direccioun
For to eschewe the flatri odious
And the fals fraude off wommen lecherous.

Wher was ther evere off science or cunnyng
So renommed as was kyng Salamoun?
Yit wommen made hym, thoruh ther fals flateryng,
To foreyn goddis doon oblacioun,
Which clipsid his honour and brouht his fame doun,
That was in wisdam whilom most vertuous,
Til he thoruh wommen fill to be lecherous.

Is it nat eek remembrid be writyng,
Off Israel how the cheeffe champioun,
Which goddis peeple hadde in his ledyng,
I meene the famous, myhti, strong Sampsoun,
That thoruh his force to-rente the lyoun, –
But Dalida with teres plenteuous
His grace berafft hym and made hym lecherous?

Lydgate's Fall of Princes, ed. cit. Book III, lines 1576–1603.

[1] amends

NINE

Later Versions

From the Story of Carados – the Prose Version

In the month of May this feast, for which God had prepared a
day so beautiful that no-one could know how to describe it, was
held; and on this day the king went to hear mass. And among the
lords of his realm, Carados was considered the most handsome of
all, and of most perfect bearing; he was among the fifty young
squires all of whom the king had made knights that day in his
honour – sons of barons, of counts, and of other great lords – all
courteous and well-bred, who had washed and bathed as was
then the custom. Guenevere the famous queen showed herself
very liberal on this day; she sent to Carados and to his
companions fine shirts richly embroidered and gave them such
robes that mighty kings might have been well dressed in them,
and in the same way she sent them very rich and beautiful cloaks,
all furred with sables and embroidered with gold stars on the
outside. The story tells us that when Carados, adorned in his rich
robes, appeared he looked so handsome that it was quite clear to
everyone that in him nature had not forgotten or left out
anything, because there was nothing in his person that could
offend or displease. And when they came to make them knights,
Gawain put on Carados's right spur and Sir Yvain the left, and
the King made the sign of the cross with the sword and then gave
him the accolade, praying to God to make him a brave and
chivalrous knight. And then this was done. A hundred of the
most highly esteemed knights of the court had fastened on the
spurs of the other fifty squires, made the sign of the cross with
their swords, and then given them the accolade. So they were

made knights, and they all went together to the church to hear the divine service which the Archbishop of Canterbury, who also performed the office of the mass of the Holy Spirit, celebrated. And you may be sure that the offering offered by every person there was great and rich. That day the king wore a crown that was worth a great treasure. When the divine service was finally concluded, the king accompanied by his nobles retired to his hall in great joy and happiness, and there the sergeants and squires prepared all the tables and the cloths, on which they set salt and bread, and on which there were dishes so rich that each one was beyond price. And while the tables were being prepared, the king with his barons and the new knights walked about outside the hall. And then Kay the Seneschal came out from a room and approached the king bare-headed, holding the bowl all ready in his hand, to ask him if it was his pleasure to wash.

'Kay,' said the king, 'don't hurry, because you know that, for a long time past, whenever I have held a full court, I never wish to eat until new or marvellous tidings are brought to me, and I do not wish to give up or abolish the custom yet.'

While they talked together there, it was announced that a knight who rode in very great haste had come through the door. And he came singing a song very sweetly, and had on his hat a circlet from which hung a wreath of flowers, and he was dressed in green satin furred with ermine. He was girded with a sword with which later his head was cut off, and which had fringes to the belt of fine silk embroidered with gold and thick with pearls scattered on top. When he came before the king he very humbly greeted him in this manner:

'Sir,' he said, 'I greet you, as the best and noblest king who reigns on this earth at the present time. Know that I come to you to ask a boon, if it may please you to grant it to me.'

'Friend,' said the king, 'I grant it to you, provided that the granting of the boon you ask of me is reasonable.'

'King,' he said, 'I do not intend to deceive anyone and the boon that I ask of you is only a blow for a blow, or, in other words, to take a blow for another blow given.'

'What do you mean by that, I should like to know?' said the king.

'Sir, I will explain,' said the knight. 'This sword, before your royal majesty and before the whole company, I shall present to a knight, if he can cut off my head with one stroke; and when I have recovered from the stroke I shall return him the blow.'

'Good God,' Kay said to himself, 'I would not undertake this thing for all the possessions that there are in the world, and I should reckon the knight who undertakes it a fool.'

And then the knight said:

'Sir,' he said, 'I have asked you a boon, and if you were to refuse me, it would be said by everyone that I should have failed, at your great feast, to obtain of you a boon which I asked of you; and therefore I beseech you, do not refuse it to me, since you cannot be blamed for it.'

Then he drew the sword from the sheath and flourished it to and fro, at which the king was very angry, and those of high rank as well as those of low estate were dumbfounded, thinking in their hearts of what honour one could win by striking and cutting off his head. Then Carados the new knight could not restrain himself from coming to present himself to satisfy the request of the knight, and as soon as he came near, he laid his cloak down and took the sword that the knight was holding. And the knight asked him:

'Are you,' he said, 'chosen as one of the best?'

'No,' said Carados, 'but as one of the most foolish.'

Then the knight stretched out his neck, laying it on a table, at which the king and all the barons in the court were much distressed, and in a moment they thought that Yvain would have run to him to take the sword from his hands. Then Carados, persisting with his intention, raised the sword that he held, with which he gave the knight such a blow that it sliced right through to the table, and the head flew further than a lance's length, and the body, just as if it were alive, followed so closely upon the head that no-one could prevent the head being replaced, well joined and well fixed on. And then the knight went to his place, saying to the king:

'Sir,' he said, 'now you must grant me my right; and on account of this blow that I have received in your court, it must be agreed only just that it should be returned, and I make you the judge of this. But I very much wish to postpone the date from today until you hold full court in a year's time.'

And then, without further delay, the king invited all the barons to come back in a year's time on the day assigned by the knight for him to return the blow. And as soon as the knight had remounted he spoke to Carados.

'Carados,' he said, 'you have given me a great blow in the presence of the king, but I call upon you a year from today to receive mine.'

And with that he left, and went on his way. And the king was in such a state of anger that no-one would know how to describe it to you, wondering how Carados could come off alive from this affair, and he fell into a grief so very great that no-one knew how to draw him out of it. And I assure you that there were no knights and ladies who did not burst into tears because of the sorrow and fear that they felt for Carados. Indeed, all the laughter and fun was turned into weeping and lamentation. Oh how hateful he is, who by his blow and by his foolish game causes everyone such grief and misery: in the end one pleasure is turned into a hundred pains. Oh detestable and more than mad enchanter, how is it that you have dared to perpetrate so wicked a crime, from which must follow so grievous a loss to your own blood and to her whom you have so much loved? When the wizard knight, whom no-one knew, had gone back, the king and the barons sat down at the table where all the talk was only of this matter, and again and again they sighed deeply. But Carados did not care at all, saying that he would see how things turned out.

Many tears were shed for Carados at Carlisle, where the barons were to re-assemble next year on the day of Pentecost. And this news was heard by Carados King of Vienne and by his wife the beautiful Ysenne, who felt great sorrow in their hearts for the danger of their child, which never ceased the whole year. And the young Carados, waiting for the year to pass and be completed, did not want to remain in his uncle the king's court; but the story tells us that he did such chivalrous deeds that no knight living on earth performed so many in such a short time, so that his renown was so great everywhere that everyone thought that his deeds were done more by divine power than by bodily means. And when he saw that the time approached for the court to re-assemble, he went straight back to Carlisle, where all the men and women who were invited to come to see the adventure were. But neither King Carados nor his wife had come there at this time, for they dared not come because of the fear and grief which they felt for their child; they scarcely had any joy while the court was being held, and they did not know any saint to pray to other than God, for prayers to whom they gave splendid and great alms, to preserve their child and keep him from death.

How the wizard knight who was the father of Carados came at the year's end pretending he meant to cut off the head of the said Carados his son.

When the court was assembled at Carlisle, on the day of Pentecost, the processions were done and the masses sung in the churches, and just when it was time to give the word to the king to go and eat, the knight appeared in the hall exactly as before; he had drawn his sword, so that he seemed to be in a great hurry, and ready to carry out his intention. He addressed the king in a simple greeting as soon as he had saluted him.

'Sir,' he said, 'if it pleases you, you will now make Carados appear here, just as it was agreed a year ago.'

And while he was saying this, he saw Carados to whom he said:

'Carados, put your head here, because you know that I put mine there and so you must put yours there. And by this means you will recognise that I know how to strike with a sword, as I give you your blow.'

Then Carados waited no longer and came and sprang forward, then put his head on the block and said to the knight:

'Come on,' he said. 'You see me! Do the worst that you can.'

Then the king called to the knight and said:

'Knight,' he said, 'I beg you to show yourself courteous; set Carados at ransom.'

'And for what?' said the knight.

'I shall give you gladly indeed,' the king said, 'all the plate that you can find in my court, that anyone has brought there, whether it belongs to me or to anyone else, with all the armour of Carados, who is my rightful nephew.'

And he said that he would take nothing, but that he would cut off his head. Then the king said to him,

'I will give you all the treasures, whether in precious stones or in anything else, that are here now in this land, both in England and in Brittany, and throughout my realms.'

'Indeed,' said the knight, 'I want none of it, but I am going to cut off his head.'

And then he lifted his sword to strike him, at which the king was deeply grieved. And Carados said to him angrily:

'Why don't you strike, noble sir? You make me die two deaths. It looks as if you are a coward, you make so much fuss about striking.'

Then the queen came out of her room with the ladies and young girls, to beg him to have pity on Carados. Then she said to him:

'I beg you, noble knight,' she said, 'not to touch Carados, because it would be a very great sin and shame if he were to be killed at this moment. For God's sake have mercy on him and I promise you that if you excuse him his death, you will receive a good reward. Believe me, I beg you, and if ever you have wished to do me any good for God's sake, I beseech you to do this for me and release my nephew from the blow that you claim you owe him. You see how many ladies and pure maidens are begging you to do this.'

'Lady,' the knight replied, 'for all the women in the world I would not consent to pardon him, because I want him to lose his life. If you can't bear to look, go and hide in your room.'

Then the queen with her head bowed retired to her room with her ladies, where they gave way to their great grief and sorrow for Carados, whom they did not know how to save.

How King Arthur with his knights, ladies and maidens were in great sorrow for fear of the death of young Carados and how the wizard knight declared openly to the said Carados that he was his son.

The king and all the knights were inflamed with very great anger because they did not know what was going to happen, and I do not believe that a mortal man has ever seen such grief expressed. Then Carados freely put his head once more upon the block, his neck stretched out, to suit the knight. And he raised the sword, only using the flat, and then said to him:

'Carados,' he said, 'now get up, for it would be a great outrage and shame if I had killed you, but I want to talk to you in private.'

And when they had gone to one side, he spoke to him like this:

'Do you know why I didn't kill you?' he said. 'It is because I am your father and you are my natural son.'

'Indeed,' said Carados, 'I shall defend my mother from that by insisting that she never was your lover and that you never lay with her, and so I beg you to be silent.'

And then the knight told Carados every detail of how this all came about, and how he lay with his mother for three nights. But Carados, who did not believe him, wanted to contradict the knight when he told him something so strange and so unexpected;

he was so sad and so grieved about this that he told him he was a liar several times and said that he would have it denied. But the knight was annoyed by nothing that Carados could say and without discussing the matter further he mounted his horse again, then took his leave and went on his way, so that he left the court in joy, when they saw Carados safe. Then Kay had the trumpets sound for the dishes to be served, and the king and the barons to wash and sit down at the table, to which came the ladies, young women and maidens, very happy at the outcome of Carados's adventure. And when they were all seated at the table, they were served with the most costly and delicious dishes, which I shall not describe in detail to you for the sake of brevity and for fear of lengthening my story. When the barons had risen after this delightful meal, they all went off to rest for the night, and the next day after mass, everyone came to the king to take his leave. But before they went, the king rewarded them with splendid gifts such as horses, rings, jewels, gold and silver, and fine hawks. Then there was no-one who came to the court poor, who did not go home rich. Each one went back to his country happily, and the king remained there with his personal household and amused himself very happily with his knights. And Carados went off to Brittany where he had not been for a long time and travelled so fast that he soon came to Nantes where he found his father the king, staying with his mother, the beautiful Ysenne.

From *Tresplaisonte et Recreative Hystoire du Trespreulx et Vaillant Chevallier Perceval le Galloys.* Avec Privilege . . . Jehan longis et Jehan sainct denis. Paris 1530. Folios, LXXXIX–CL.
In L.D. Benson: *Art and Tradition in Sir Gawain and the Green Knight*, New Brunswick, 1965, pp. 250–7.

The Grene Knight

List! wen Arthur he was King,
he had all att his leadinge
 the broad Ile of Brittaine;
England and Scotland one was,
and wales stood in the same case,
 the truth itt is not to layne.

he drive allyance out of this Ile,
soe Arthur lived in peace a while,
 as man of Mickle maine,
knights strong of their degree
[strove] which of them hyest shold bee;
 therof Arthur was not faine;

hee made the round table for their behove,
that none of them shold sitt above,
 but all shold sitt as one,
the King himselfe in state royall,
Dame Guenever our queene withall,
 seemlye of body and bone.

itt fell againe the christmase,
many came to that Lords place,
 to that worthye one
with helme on head, and brand bright,
all that tooke order of knight;
 none wold linger att home.

there was noe castle nor manour free
that might harbour that companye,
 their puissance was soe great.
their tents up they pight
for to lodge there all that night,
 therto were sett to meate.

The Green Knight

LISTEN! When Arthur was king he had all the broad island of Britain under his control. England and Scotland were united, and Wales was in the same state, a truth not to be denied.

Arthur drove his enemies out of this island, so, as a man of great strength, he lived in peace for a while. Arthur was not fond of knights contending in their rank as to which of them should be highest.

He made the Round Table for their benefit, so that none of them should be seated above the other, but all should sit equal, the king himself in royal state and Dame Guenevere our queen, so lovely in every way, with them.

It happened one Christmas that many people came to the place of that lord, that noble one, with helmets on heads and bright swords, all who held the order of knighthood, for no-one would stay at home.

There was no castle nor noble manor that could hold that company, they came in such great strength. They pitched their tents so as to lodge there all night, and then sat down to eat.

Messengers there came [and] went
with much victualls verament
    both by way and streete;
wine and wild fowle thither was brought,
within they spared nought
    for gold, and they might itt gett.

Now of King Arthur noe more I mell;
but of a venterous knight I will you tell
    that dwelled in the west countrye;
Sir Bredbeddle, for sooth he hett;
he was a man of Mickele might,
    and Lord of great bewtye.

he had a lady to his wiffe,
he loved her deerlye as his liffe,
    shee was both blyth and blee;
because Sir Gawaine was stiffe in stowre,
shee loved him privilye paramour,
    and shee never him see.

itt was Agostes that was her mother;
itt was witchcraft and noe other
    that shee dealt with all;

shee cold transpose knights and swaine
like as in battaile they were slaine,
    wounded both Lim and lightt,
shee taught her sonne the Knight alsoe
in transposed likenesse he shold goe
    both by fell and frythe;

shee said, 'thou shalt to Arthurs hall;
for there great adventures shall befall
    That ever saw King or Knight.'
all was for her daughters sake,
that which she soe sadlye spake
    to her sonne-in-law the Knight,
because Sir Gawaine was bold and hardye,
and therto full of curtesye,
    to bring him into her sight.

Messengers came and went both by road and through the streets with a great deal of food, in truth. Wine and wildfowl were brought in, and nothing was spared there that could be bought for gold, if they could get it.

Now I shall say no more of King Arthur, but I shall tell you of a knight errant who lived in the west country. He was called Sir Bredbeddle, in fact, and was a man of great strength and also most handsome.

His wife was a lady, and he loved her as dearly as his own life, for she was both merry and beautiful. Because Sir Gawain was strong in battle she secretly loved him as her love, although she had never seen him.

Agostes was her mother, and she worked with witchcraft and nothing else.

(3 *lines missing*.)

She could change knights, as if they had been slain in battle, wounded both in limb and body, into peasants. She taught her son-in-law the knight, too, so that he could go about in changed appearance, both by field and wood.

She said:
   'You shall go to Arthur's hall, for there greater adventures shall happen to you, than ever king or knight saw.'

(3 *lines missing*.)

All that the witch said so seriously to her son-in-law the knight was for her daughter's sake, to bring Sir Gawain, who was so brave and strong and also full of courtesy, into her presence.

the knight said 'soe mote I thee,
to Arthurs court will I mee hye
   for to praise thee right,
and to prove Gawaines points three;
and that be true that men tell me,
   by Mary Most of Might.'

earlye, soone as itt was day,
the Knight dressed him full gay,
   umstrode a full good steede;
helme and hawberke both he hent,
a long fauchion verament
   to fend them in his neede.

that was a Jolly sight to seene,
when horsse and armour was all greene,
   and weapon that hee bare.
when that burne was harnisht still,
his countenance he became right well,
   I dare itt safelye sweare.

that time att Carleile lay our King;
att a Castle of flatting was his dwelling,
   in the fforrest of delamore.
for sooth he rode, the sooth to say,
to Carleile he came on Christmas day,
   into that fayre countrye.

when he into that place came,
the porter thought him a Marvelous groome;
   he saith, 'Sir, wither wold yee?'
hee said, 'I am a venterous Knight,
and of your King wold have sight,
   and other Lords that heere bee.'

noe word to him the porter spake,
but left him standing att the gate,
   and went forth, as I weene,
and kneeled downe before the King;
saith, 'in lifes dayes old or younge,
   such a sight I have not seene!

The knight replied:

'As I hope to thrive, I will hurry to Arthur's court, to praise you suitably, and to prove Gawain's three qualities, if what I hear is true, by Mary of greatest might.'

Early, as soon as it was day, the knight dressed himself brightly and mounted a very good horse. He took his helmet and his coat of mail, and a long falchion, too, to defend himself in his need.

It was a pleasant sight to see, since horse and armour were all green, as well as the weapons that he bore. When the warrior was completely armed his appearance suited him very well, I dare safely swear.

At that time our king was at Carlisle: his residence was at a castle at Flatting in the Forest of Delamore. And to tell you the whole truth, the knight rode and came to Carlisle on Christmas day, riding through that beautiful countryside.

When he came to that place the porter thought him an extraordinary man and he said:

'Sir, where do you wish to go?'

He replied:

'I am a knight errant and I wish to see your king and the other lords that are here.'

The porter spoke never a word to him, but left him standing at the gate and went away, I am told, and kneeled down before the king and said:

'In all the days of my life, old or young, I have never seen such a sight,

'for yonder att your gates right;'
he saith, 'there is a venterous Knight;
   all his vesture is greene.'
then spake the King proudest in all,
saith, 'bring him into the hall;
   let us see what hee doth meane.'

when the greene Knight came before the King,
he stood in his stirrops strechinge,
   and spoke with voice cleere,
and saith, 'King Arthur, god save thee
as thou sittest in thy prosperitye,
   and Maintaine thine honor!

'why thou wold me nothing but right;
I am come hither a venterous [Knight,]
   and kayred thorrow countrye farr,
to prove poynts in thy pallace
that longeth to manhood in everye case
   among thy Lords deere.'

the King, he sayd full still
till he had said all his will;
   certein thus can he say:
'as I am true knight and King,
thou shalt have thy askinge!
   I will not say thy nay,

'whether thou wilt on foote fighting,
or on steed backe justing
   for love of Ladyes gay.
If and thine armor be not fine,
I will give thee part of mine.'
   'god amercy, Lord!' can he say,

'here I make a challenging
among the Lords both old and younge
   that worthy beene in weede,
which of them will take in hand –
hee that is both stiffe and stronge
   and full good att need –

for there right outside your gates – there is a knight errant – all his clothes are green!' he said.

Then the king in his splendid array spoke, saying:

'Bring him into the hall. Let us see what his intention is.'

When the Green Knight came before the king, he stood right up in his stirrups and spoke in a clear voice and said:

'God save you, King Arthur, as you sit in your prosperity and maintain your honour.

While you wish me nothing but right, I have come here, a knight errant, and ridden through far countries to test some of the qualities that in every instance belong to manhood, among your beloved lords in your palace.'

The king sat very still until he had had his say and then he certainly answered like this:

'As I am a true knight and king, you shall have your request. I will not deny you.

Do you want to fight on foot or joust on horse-back for the love of beautiful ladies? If your armour is not good enough I will give you some of mine.'

'Thank you, my lord,' he replied.

'I here offer a challenge among the lords, both old and young, that are worthy in their array: which of them will take on a man who is both brave and strong and very good at need?

'I shall lay my head downe,
strike itt of if he can
 with a stroke to garr itt bleed,
for this day twelve monthe another at his:
let me see who will answer this,
 a knight that is doughtye of deed;

'for this day twelve month, the sooth to say,
let him come to me and seicth his praye;
 rudlye, or ever hee blin,
whither to come, I shall him tell,
the readie way to the greene chappell,
 that place I will be in.'

the King att ease sate full still,
and all his lords said but litle
 till he had said all his will.
upp stood Sir Kay that crabbed knight,
spake mightye words that were of height,
 that were both Loud and shrill;

'I shall strike his necke in tooe,
the head away the body froe.'
 they bade him all be still,
saith, 'Kay, of thy dints make noe rouse,
thou wottest full litle what thou does;
 noe good, but Mickle ill.'

Eche man wold this deed have done.
up start Sir Gawaine soone,
 upon his knees can kneele,
he said, 'that were great villanye
without you put this deede to me,
 my leege, as I have sayd;

'remember, I am your sisters sonne.'
the King said, 'I grant thy boone;
 but mirth is best att meele;
cheere thy guest, and give him wine,
and after dinner, to itt fine,
 and sett the buffett well!'

I shall lay my head down: let him strike it off, if he can, with a stroke to make it bleed, in exchange for another to his head this day twelve-month. Let me see who will answer this: a knight that is brave in action.

This day twelve-month let him come to me and fetch his pay, promptly without hesitation. I shall tell him where to come, the easy way to the Green Chapel – that's the place I shall be in.'

The king, at his ease, sat very still, and all his lords said very little, till he had said all he wished to say. Then up stood that ill-tempered knight, Sir Kay, and spoke boastful and high-sounding words, that were both loud and shrill.

'I shall strike his neck in two, and the head away from the body.'
They all told him to be quiet. They said:
'Kay, make no boast of your blows. You are very little aware of what you are doing: no good but a great deal of evil.'

Each man would have taken him on immediately. Sir Gawain got up and kneeled down on his knees. He said:
'It would be quite shameful if you did not assign this deed to me, my liege, as I have said.

Remember I am your sister's son.'
The king said:
'I grant your request, but merriment is best at mealtimes. Cheer your guest and give him wine, and after dinner finish it off, and place the stroke well.'

now the greene Knight is set att meate,
seemlye served in his seate,
   beside the round table.
to talke of his welfare, nothing he needs,
like a Knight himselfe he feeds,
   with long time reasnable.

when the dinner, it was done,
the King said to Sir Gawaine soone,
   withouten any fable
he said, 'on you will doe this deede,
I pray Jesus be your speede!
   this knight is nothing unstable.'

the greene Knight his head downe layd;
Sir Gawaine, to the axe he braid
   to strike with eger will;
he stroke the necke bone in twaine,
the blood burst out in everye vaine,
   the head from the body fell.

the greene Knight his head up hent,
into his saddle wightilye he sprent,
   spake words both Lowd and shrill,
saith: 'Gawaine! thinke on thy covenant!
this day twelve monthes see thou ne want
   to come to the greene chappell!'

All had great marvell, that they see
that he spake so merrilye
   and bare his head in his hand.
forth att the hall dore he rode right,
and that saw both king and knight
   and Lords that were in land.

without the hall dore, the sooth to saine,
hee sett his head upon againe,
   saies, 'Arthur, have heere my hand!
when-soever the Knight cometh to mee,
a better buffett sickerlye
   I dare him well warrand.'

The Green Knight now sat down to dinner, and was suitably served in his place at the Round Table. As far as his well-being is concerned, there is nothing that he needs. He feeds himself like a knight, taking a reasonably long time.

When the dinner was done, the king at once said to Sir Gawain, without any deception:

'If you will do this deed, I pray to Jesus to help you, for this knight is not at all changeable.'

The Green Knight laid down his head, and Sir Gawain took the axe to strike with eager will. He struck the neck-bone in two – the blood burst out from every vein – the head fell from the body.

The Green Knight caught up his head and vigorously sprang into his saddle, and spoke both loud and piercing words: he said:

'Gawain, remember your agreement. See that you do not fail to come to the Green Chapel this day twelve-month.'

All were very astonished when they saw that he spoke so merrily and carried his head in his hand. He rode right out of the hall door and both the king and the knights and the lords who were in that land saw it.

Outside the hall door, to tell the truth, he put his head back on again and said:

'Arthur, take my hand here. Whenever the knight comes to me, I shall give him a better blow without a doubt, I dare warrant him well.'

the greene Knight away went.
all this was done by enchantment
 that the old witch had wrought.
sore sicke fell Arthur the King,
and for him made great mourning
 that into such bale was brought.

the Queen, shee weeped for his sake;
sorry was Sir Lancelott dulake,
 and other were dreery in thought
because he was brought into great perill;
his mightye manhood will not availe,
 that before hath freshlye fought.

Sir Gawaine comfort King and Queen,
and all the doughtye there be-deene;
 he bade they shold be still;
said, 'of my deede I was never feard,
nor yett I am nothing a-dread,
 I swere by Saint Michaell;

'for when draweth toward my day,
I will dresse me in mine array
 my promise to fulfill.
Sir,' he saith, 'as I have blis,
I wott not where the greene chappell is,
 therfore seeke itt I will.'

the royall Courtt verament
all rought Sir Gawaines intent,
 they thought itt was the best.
they went forth into the feild,
knights that ware both speare and sheeld
 they pric[k]ed forth full prest;

some chuse them to Justinge,
some to dance, Revell, and sing;
 of mirth they wold not rest.
all they swore together in fere,
that and Sir Gawaine over-come were,
 they wold bren all the west.

The Green Knight went away. All this was done by the enchantment that the old witch had brought about. King Arthur became very ill, and great sorrow was made for him, as he was brought into such distress.

The queen wept for his sake, and Sir Lancelot du Lake was sorry, and the others were very miserable. The strength of his manhood that had fought so strongly before could not help, because he was brought into great danger.

Sir Gawain comforted the king and queen and all the brave ones there besides, and insisted that they should be calm. He said:
  'I have never been afraid in consequence of what I have done, nor am I in the least frightened now, I swear by St. Michael.

For when it comes to the time I shall put on all my equipment, so as to fulfil my promise. As I hope for heaven, sir, I don't know where the Green Chapel is, and so I shall search for it.'

The royal court all carried out Sir Gawain's wish, in truth - they thought it was for the best. They went off to the field, knights bearing spears and shields, riding off in great haste.

Some chose to do jousting, some to dance, revel and sing. They would not leave off their merriment. They all swore to one another together that if Sir Gawain were overcome, they would set fire to all the west country.

Now leave wee the King in his pallace.
the greene Knight come home is
 to his owne Castle;
this folke frend when he came home
what doughtye deeds he had done.
 nothing he wold them tell;

full well hee wist in certaine
that his wiffe loved Sir Gawaine
 that comelye was under kell.
listen, Lords! and yee will sitt,
and yee shall heere the second ffitt,
 what adventures Sir Gawaine befell.

[Part II]

The day is come that Gawaine must gone;
Knights and Ladyes waxed wann
 that were without in that place;
the King himselfe siked ill,
the Queen a swounding almost fell
 to that Jorney when he shold passe.

When he was in armour bright,
he was one of the goodlyest Knights
 that ever in brittaine was borne.
they brought Sir Gawaine a steed
was dapple gray and good att need,
 I tell withouten scorne;

his bridle was with stones sett,
with gold and pearle overfrett,
 and stones of great vertue;
he was of a furley kind;
his stirropps were of silke of ynd;
 I tell you this tale for true.

when he rode over the Mold,
his geere glistered as gold.
 by the way as he rode,
many furley he there did see,
fowles by the water did flee,
 by brimes and bankes soe broad.

Now let us leave the king in his palace. The Green Knight has come home to his own castle. When he came home, his people asked what brave deeds he had done, but he would tell them nothing.

He knew very well for a fact, that his wife loved Sir Gawain – his beautiful wife. Listen, lords, if you will sit still, and you shall hear the second part of the adventures that happened to Sir Gawain.

[Second part]

The day is come for Gawain to go. The knights and ladies who were about the place grew pale. The king sighed bitterly. The queen almost fell fainting when he had to go off on that journey.

When he was in his shining armour he was one of the goodliest knights that was ever born in Britain. They brought Sir Gawain a dapple-grey horse which was good at time of need, I can tell you without question.

His bridle was set with jewels and ornamented with gold and pearl, and with jewels of great power. His appearance was marvellous, and his stirrups were of Indian silk. This tale that I am telling you is true.

His armour shone like gold as he rode over the ground, as he rode by the way. He saw many wonders there, and birds flew near the water, by the brinks and banks that were so broad.

many furleys there saw hee
of wolves and wild beasts sikerlye;
     on hunting hee tooke most heede.
forth he rode, the sooth to tell,
for to seeke the greene chappell,
     he wist not where indeed.

As he rode in an evening late,
riding downe a greene gate,
     a faire castell saw hee,
that seemed a place of Mickle pride;
thitherward Sir Gawaine can ryde
     to gett some harborrowe.

thither he came in the twylight,
he was ware of a gentle Knight,
     the Lord of the place was hee.
Meekly to him Sir Gawaine can speake,
and asked him, 'for King Arthurs sake,
     of harborrowe I pray thee!

'I am a far Labordd Knight,
I pray you lodge me all this night.'
     he sayd him not nay,
hee tooke him by the arme and led him to the hall.
a poore child can hee call,
     saith, 'dight well this palfrey.'

into a chamber they went a full great speed;
there they found all things readye att need,
     I dare safelye swere;
fier in chambers burning bright,
candles in chandlers burning light;
     to supper they went full yare.

he sent after his Ladye bright
to come to supp with that gentle Knight,
     and shee came blythe with-all;
forth shee came then anon,
her Maids following her eche one
     in robes of rich pall.

He saw many wonders such as wolves and wild beasts, indeed, and he took much care about hunting. To tell you the truth, he rode out to search for the Green Chapel, although he did not know where it was.

As he rode late one evening, riding down a green path, he saw a fine castle. It seemed a place of great pride, and Gawain rode towards it to get some shelter.

He came to it in the twilight; he became aware of a noble knight – the lord of the place he was. Sir Gawain spoke humbly to him, requesting him for King Arthur's sake to give him shelter.

'I am a far-travelled knight, and beg you to give me lodging for this night'
He did not refuse him. He took him by the arm and led him to the hall, then called a poor child, and said:
'Look after his palfrey well.'

They went swiftly into a room where they found everything ready as required, I dare safely swear. Fires were burning in the rooms and candles in the candlesticks giving light, so they went very eagerly to supper.

He sent for his beautiful lady to come and have supper with the noble knight and she came with great happiness. She soon came along, then, with every one of her maids following her in gowns of rich material.

as shee sate att her supper,
ever-more the Ladye clere
   Sir Gawaine shee looked upon.
when the supper it was done,
shee tooke her Maids, and to her chamber gone.

he cheered the Knight and gave him wine,
and said, 'welcome, by St Martine!
   I pray you take itt for none ill;
one thing, Sir, I wold you pray;
what you make soe farr this way?
   the truth you wold me tell;

'I am a Knight, and soe are yee;
Your concell, an you will tell mee,
   forsoothe keepe itt I will;
for if itt be poynt of any dread,
perchance I may helpe att need
   either lowd or still.'

for his words that were soe smooth,
had Sir Gawaine wist the soothe,
   all he wold not have told,
for that was the greene Knight
that hee was lodged with that night,
   and harbarrowes in his hold.

he saith, 'as to the greene chappell,
thitherward I can you tell,
   itt is but furlongs three.
the Master of it is a venterous Knight,
and workes by witchcraft day and knight,
   with many a great furley.

'if he worke with never soe much frauce,
he is curteous as he sees cause.
   I tell you sikerlye,
you shall abyde, and take your rest,
and I will into yonder fforest
   under the greenwood tree.'

As she sat at her supper, the lovely lady gazed at Sir Gawain all the time. When the supper was done, she took all her maids with her and went to her room.

The host cheered the knight and gave him wine, and said:
'Welcome, by St. Martin! I beg you not to take it ill; but one thing I must ask you, sir, – that you would tell me the truth about what makes you come so far this way.

I am a knight, and so are you. If you will tell me what is in your mind, I will certainly keep it secret; for if it is any matter for anxiety, perhaps I can help at need, whatever it may be.'

If Sir Gawain had known the truth, he would not have told him anything for all his smooth talk. For it was the Green Knight that he was lodged with that night, and in whose castle he was staying.

He said:
'As to the Green Chapel, I can tell you the way there. It is only three furlongs. The master of it is a daring knight who works by witchcraft all the time, producing many a wonder.

However hard he works, he is courteous when he sees fit, I can certainly assure you. You shall stay here and rest, and I shall go into the forest out there, under the greenwood tree.'

they plight their truthes to beleeve,
either with other for to deale,
    whether it were silver or gold;
he said, 'we two both sworn wilbe,
what soever god sends you and mee,
    to be parted on the Mold.'

The greene Knight went on hunting;
Sir Gawaine in the castle beinge,
    lay sleeping in his bed.
Uprose the old witche with hast throwe,
and to her daughter can shee goe,
    and said, 'be not adread!'

to her daughter can shee say,
'the man that thou hast wisht many a day,
    of him thou maist be sped;
for Sir Gawaine that curteous Knight
is lodged in this hall all night.'
    shee brought her to his bedd.

shee saith, 'gentle Knight, awake!
and for this faire Ladies sake
    that hath loved thee soe deere,
take her boldly in thine armes,
there is noe man shall doe thee harme;'
    now beene they both heere.

the ladye kissed him times three,
saith, 'without I have the love of thee,
    my life standeth in dere.'
Sir Gawaine blushed on the Lady bright,
saith, 'your husband is a gentle Knight,
    by him that bought mee deare!

'to me itt were great shame
if I shold doe him any grame,
    that hath beene kind to mee;
for I have such a deede to doe,
that I can neyther rest nor roe,
    att an end till itt bee.'

They give their promises to be loyal in sharing with each other, whether it should be silver or gold. He said:

'We will both be true, whatever God sends us to be divided between us on earth.'

The Green Knight went hunting, Sir Gawain staying in the castle and lying asleep in his bed. Up rose the old witch in haste, then, and she went to her daughter and said:

'Don't be afraid.'

She said to her daughter:

'You may now succeed with the man that you have wished for for many a day; for Sir Gawain, that courteous knight, is staying in this hall all night long.'

She brought her to his bed.

She says:

'Noble knight, awake, and for the sake of this fair lady who has loved you so dearly, take her boldly in your arms – there is no man who can do you harm.'

Now they were both together.

The lady kissed him three times. She said:

'Unless I have your love, my life will be in danger.'

Sir Gawain looked at the lovely lady, and said:

'Your husband is a noble knight, by him who redeemed me at such cost.

It would be very shameful of me if I were to do him any injury, for he has been kind to me. But I have such a deed to do that I can neither rest nor enjoy myself until it is done.'

then spake that Ladye gay,
saith, 'tell me some of your Journey,
 your succour I may bee;
if itt be poynt of any warr,
there shall noe man doe you noe darr
 and yee wilbe governed by mee;

'for heere I have a lace of silke,
it is as white as any milke,
 and of a great value.'
shee saith, 'I dare safelye sweare
there shall noe man doe you deere
 when you have it upon you.'

Sir Gawaine spake mildlye in the place,
he thanked the Lady and tooke the lace,
 and promised her to come againe.
the Knight in the fforest slew many a hind,
other venison he cold none find
 but wild bores on the plaine.

plentye of does and wild swine,
foxes and other ravine,
 as I hard true men tell.
Sir Gawaine swore sickerlye
'home to your owne, welcome you bee,
 by him that harrowes hell!'

the greene Knight his venison downe Layd;
then to Sir Gawaine thus hee said,
 'tell me anon in heght,
what noveltyes that you have won,
for heers plenty of venison.'
 Sir Gawaine said full right,

Sir Gawaine sware by St Leonard,
'such as god sends, you shall have part:'
 in his armes he hent the Knight,
and there he kissed him times three,
saith, 'heere is such as god sends mee,
 by Mary most of Might.'

Then that elegant lady spoke and said:

'Tell me about your travels, so that I can be of help to you; if it is a matter of any fighting, no man shall do you any injury if you will be governed by me.

For I have here a silken lace, as white as milk, and of great value. I can safely swear that no man shall do you an injury when you have it on you,' she said.

Sir Gawain spoke gently to her there, thanked the lady and took the lace, promising her to come again. The knight killed many a hind in the forest; but he could find no other game, only wild boars on the plain.

Plenty of does and wild pigs, foxes and other vermin, as I have heard true men say. Sir Gawain greeted him confidently:

'You are welcome to your own home, by Him that harrows hell.'

The Green Knight laid down his venison and then he said to Sir Gawain:

'Tell me at once, truly, what new things you have won, for here is plenty of venison.'

Sir Gawain readily complied.

Sir Gawain swore by St Leonard:

'Such as God sends, you shall have a share of.'

He took the knight in his arms and there he kissed him three times. He said:

'Here is what God has sent me, by Mary, greatest in power.'

ever privily he held the lace:
that was all the villanye that ever was
   prooved by Sir Gawaine the gay.
then to bed soone they went,
and sleeped there verament
   till morrow itt was day.

then sir Gawaine soe curteous and free
his leave soone taketh hee
   att the Lady soe gaye;
Hee thanked her, and tooke the lace,
and rode towards the chappell apace;
   he knew noe whitt the way.

ever more in his thought he had
whether he shold worke as the Ladye bade,
   that was soe curteous and sheene.
the greene knight rode another way;
he transposed him in another array,
   before as it was greene.

as Sir Gawaine rode over the plaine,
he hard on high upon a Mountaine
   a horne blowne full lowde.
he looked after the greene chappell,
he saw itt stand under a hill
   covered with evyes about;

he looked after the greene Knight,
he hard him whett a fauchion bright,
   that the hills rang about.
the Knight spake with strong cheere,
said, 'yee be welcome, Sir Gawaine heere,
   it behooveth thee to lowte.'
he stroke, and litle perced the skin,
unneth the flesh within.
   then Sir Gawaine had noe doubt;

He secretly kept the lace all the time. That was all the mischief that ever was performed by brave Sir Gawain. Then they promptly went to bed and slept there, in fact, until next day in the morning.

Then Sir Gawain, so courteous and noble, at once took his leave of the elegant lady; he thanked her, and took the lace, and rode rapidly towards the Chapel. He did not know the way at all.

All the time he was thinking whether he should do as the lady, who was so courteous and beautiful, told him. The Green Knight rode another way, and changed himself into another guise, green as before.

As Sir Gawain rode over the plain he heard someone high up on a mountain blow a horn very loudly;
(3 lines missing.)
He looked for the Green Chapel and saw it standing at the foot of a hill, covered all over with ivy.

He looked for the Green Knight, and heard him sharpen a bright falchion so that the hills round about rang. The knight spoke with a hearty manner and said:
'You are welcome here, Sir Gawain. Now you must bend down.'
He struck, and slightly grazed the skin, but scarcely the flesh beneath. Then Sir Gawain had no fear.

he saith, 'thou shontest! why dost thou soe?'
then Sir Gawaine in hart waxed throe;
   upon his ffeete can stand,
and soone he drew out his sword,
and saith, 'traitor! if thou speake a word,
   thy liffe is in my hand;
I had but one stroke att thee,
and thou hast had another att mee,
   noe falshood in me thou found!'

the Knight said withouten laine,
'I wend I had Sir Gawaine slaine,
   the gentlest Knight in this land;
men told me of great renowne,
of curtesie thou might have woon the crowne
   above both free and bound,

'and alsoe of great gentrye;
and now three points be put fro thee,
   it is the Moe pittye:
Sir Gawaine! thou wast not Leele
when thou didst the lace conceale
   that my wiffe gave to thee!

'ffor wee were both, thou wist full well
for thou hadst the halfe dale
   of my venerye;
if the lace had never beene wrought,
to have slaine thee was never my thought,
   I swere by god verelye!

'I wist it well my wiffe loved thee;
thou wold doe me noe villanye,
   but nicked her with nay;
but wilt thou doe as I bidd thee,
take me to Arthurs court with thee,
   then were all to my pay.'

He says:

'You are flinching: why do you do that?'

Then Sir Gawain grew angry in his heart and stood up on his feet; and immediately he drew his sword and said:

'Traitor, if you speak a word, your life is in my hand. I only aimed one stroke at you and you aimed another at me. You found no falsehood in me.'

(3 lines missing.)

The knight said:

'To tell you the truth, I thought I had killed Sir Gawain, the noblest knight in this land. Men of great renown told me that you above all others might have won the crown of courtesy,

and also of great nobility. And now three accusations are made against you, more's the pity. Sir Gawain, you were not loyal when you concealed the lace that my wife gave you.

For we were both agreed very well, and you had a half share of my hunting. If the lace had never been made, I would never have intended to kill you, I swear truly by God.

I knew well that my wife loved you; you wished to do no wrong to me, but gave her a firm refusal. But if you will do as I ask you, take me to Arthur's court with you, and then everything will be to my satisfaction.'

now are the Knights accorded there;
to the castle of hutton can they fare,
  to lodge there all that night.
earlye on the other day
to Arthurs court they tooke the way
  with harts blyth and light.

all the Court was full faine,
alive when they saw Sir Gawaine;
  they thanked god abone.
that is the matter and the case
why Knights of the bathe weare the lace
  untill they have wonen their shoen,

or else a ladye of hye estate
from about his necke shall it take,
  for the doughtye deeds that hee hath done.
it was confirmed by Arthur the King;
thorrow Sir Gawaines desiringe
  The King granted him his boone.

Thus endeth the tale of the greene Knight.
god, that is soe full of might,
  to heaven their soules bring
that have hard this litle storye
that fell some times in the west countrye
  in Arthurs days our King!

                    ffins.

From *Bishop Percy's Folio Manuscript. Ballads and Romances*, ed. John Hales and Frederick J. Furnivall, vol. II Part I, London 1867, pp. 58–77.

Now the knights have made peace there, and they go off to the Castle of Hutton to lodge there all that night. Early next day, they made their way to Arthur's court with happy, light hearts.

All the court was very glad when they saw Sir Gawain alive; they gave thanks to God above. That is the reason and the cause why Knights of the Bath wear the lace until they have won their spurs,

or until a lady of high rank takes it from a knight's neck because of the brave deeds that he has done. It was confirmed by King Arthur at Sir Gawain's desire; the king granted him his request.

So ends the tale of the Green Knight; God who is so full of power, bring their souls to heaven who have heard this little story that happened once in the west country, in the days of Arthur, our king.

Sir Gawain and the Carl of Carlisle

This romance exists in only two copies: one is MS Porkington 10 of the fifteenth century, and the other is a shorter debased version in the Percy Folio of the seventeenth century. The version in the Porkington MS is itself debased in style and eccentric in language, though it gives the fuller version of the story. Since our interest is in the story, a modern translation is given in order to save the reader the tedium of struggling with unfamiliar spelling and glosses.

Listen, my lordings, for a short while about a man who was true and strong and brave in his deeds. He was as gentle as a maiden in her bower, and yet so bold in every fight that there was no-one so valiant in action. He would go seeking feats of arms in war and peace in many a strange land, and would not be denied. Certainly, beyond a shadow of doubt, he was with King Arthur at the Round Table, as we read in the romances.

His name was Sir Gawain and he won great honour in Britain, and he was hardy and strong. (What is called the Island of Britain certainly includes Scotland and England, as it is correctly written down in history. Wales is a corner of that island.) The king was staying at Cardiff for a time, as great lords are accustomed to do, with many noble knights, with hardy and strong lords who wanted to hunt in England.

King Arthur said to his lords, as a royal master might well do:
'Let us hear mass; Bishop Baldwin shall celebrate it. Then we will go to the forest, everyone who is here now, for now is the time of year when the deer are fat and when brave barons should hunt them, and flush them from their cover.'
Sir Marrok was extremely pleased, and so was the knight Sir Kay Caradoc, and others of higher and lower rank.

Sir Lancelot du Lake was glad, and so was Sir Perceval, I assure you, and Launfal, too. So was Sir Yvain the Vyttryan and Sir Lot of Lothian, who was brave and daring, Sir Gadiffer and Sir Galeran, Sir Constantine and Sir Reinbrun, the knight with green armour. Sir Gawain was steward of the hall, and the master of them all, and hurried to get ready.

The king's uncle Sir Mordred took some noble knights with him, as one can read in the romance. The noble knight Sir Yngeles led some hounds with him that could do their work well. Sir Lybeaus Desconnu was there, with proud men of both high and low rank to make the dun deer bleed, and Sir Pettipace of Winchelsea, a noble and chivalrous knight, who was a brave man on a horse.

Sir Grandon and Sir Fair Unknown merrily followed with shouts and with their swift hounds. Sir Brandelys and Sir Ironside and many a brave man rode that day on horses that were swift and beautiful. Ironside, I believe, fathered the knight with the green armour on a lovely lady. As I understand it, it was the fair maid of Blanchland, a lovely lady in her bower.

Ironside, I understand, used to ride fully armed in the proper way however hot the sun was. In winter he bore his arms, too, and the giants and he were always at war and always fighting. His horse was called Tawny-Foot and his armour and other equipment were very handsome and costly. His coat of arms was of azure, in truth, with a beautiful griffin in gold, and set full of gold flowers.

He knew more about hunting and war than all the kings who were there. Very often he would put them to the test. He had killed fiery dragons and many a wild bull, considered frightful. He had captured great barons – a hardier knight could not be found: very courageous he was, and brave. And so, as I have heard, in his lifetime he was called the king's companion and reckoned among the brave knights.

His crest was a golden lion and his words were wise at all times; listen, and you will hear. Wherever he went, whether east or west, he lost no opportunity of fighting man or beast, whether far or near.

The eager knights rode fast, the king followed with many more men, five hundred and more, I believe. Then others, the noble archers, followed with their feathered arrows to kill the beautiful fallow deer.

The barons blew their horns, the deer came running one after another, hart and hind as well. By then it was nine o'clock, and five hundred deer lay dead in a row under a lime-tree.

Then Sir Gawain and Sir Kay and Bishop Baldwin, as I shall tell you, rode off after a reindeer. From nine o'clock until midafternoon they never stopped. A mist began to come up on the moor and the barons blew their horns fiercely. Sir Kay greatly complained because the reindeer would not stop. Listen to the adventure that befell them. They would gladly have found shelter.

Then the noble knight Sir Gawain said:

'All this labour is in vain, I am quite certain. The deer has gone quite out of view and we shall meet no more with him tonight, so gentlemen, listen to me. I suggest that we dismount from our horses and stay in the wood all night, and lie under this tree.'

'Let us ride on,' said Kay at once. 'We shall find lodging before we go much further, let no man dare to deny it me.'

Then the bishop said:

'I know very well that there is a Carl who lives in a castle very nearby. The Carl of Carlisle is his name, and by St James, he might give us lodging, I should think. There was never a man so bold who ever stayed in his castle but that he found an evil lodging. He will get beaten, I have heard it said, and if he escapes with his life, it is only through the intervention of God.

Now let all three of us ride there together.'

'I agree to that, as I hope to prosper,' said Kay. 'And as you say, it shall be done. However bold the Carl is, I don't consider him to be worth a hair and however strong he is, we will give him a good beating and lay waste his house. What he brews, he shall be made to drink, and he shall be beaten until he is a stinking corpse, and he shall stay there against his will.'

Sir Gawain replied:

'As I hope for heaven, I am not going to stay there against his will, though I could very well, if any fair words could help to make the lord glad to have us in his castle. Kay, stop your boastful behaviour. You are going out of your way to cause trouble, I tell you, as I hope for health. I shall ask the good lord as I say, for lodging until tomorrow, and for food and meals.'

They rode rapidly on their way, and halted at the castle gate, and had to call the porter. There was a hammer hanging on a chain, but Kay did not want to knock with it: he would rather have pulled the hammer off. The porter came quietly, found them there, and asked them what they wanted. Then Sir Gawain courteously said:

'We ask your lord for lodging, the noble lord of this castle.'

The porter answered them:

'I should be very glad to deliver your message; but if you suffer in consequence, don't thank me for it. You are so sound in body and limb, and handsome as well, and cheerful too, that it is good to see you. My lord knows no courtesy, and you will not get away without ill-treatment, you may believe me. I am very sorry indeed that you came this way, and before you go, you will say the same, unless there is a greater grace.'

'Porter,' said Kay, 'don't you worry. You see that we can go no further. I think you are joking. Unless you will take our message, we shall take the king's keys and pull down your gates.'

The porter said, 'As I hope to prosper, there are not three knights living who dare do that, I think. If my lord heard your boastful words, some of you would lose your lives, or else very soon be put to flight.'

The porter went into the hall, and soon found his lord, who was strong and fearless.

'Carl of Carlisle, may God save you, there are three men at the gate, fit to bear arms; two knights of Arthur's house, a bishop, and no more for certain, so they told me.'

Then the Carl said,

'By St Michael, that news greatly pleases me, since they wish to come this way.'

When they came before that Lord they found four whelps lying by his fire. They were a dreadful sight to see: a wild bull and a fierce boar, and a lion that would bite savagely, which greatly astonished them. A huge bear lay there quite unbound – such were the four whelps that they found at the Carl's knee. They rose and came up to the knights, and they would have killed them at once, but the Carl told them to leave them alone.

'Lie down, my four whelps,' he said.

Then the lion began to scowl, and he glowed like a hot coal. The bear began to growl and the bull to roar, and at once the boar whetted his tusks without a moment's delay. Then the Carl said:

'Lie still; keep down.'

They fell back for fear of him, so greatly did they dread him. At a mere word from the Carl, they crept away under the table; Sir Kay took special note of it.

The Carl looked at the knights with a stern, fierce expression; he seemed a fearsome man. With great cheeks and a broad face, an aquiline nose and generously proportioned, he had a large expanse between his brows, his mouth was huge and his beard gray. His hair lay over his breast as broad as a fan. Between his shoulders, anyone who could judge properly could see that he was two tailor's yards broad. Sir Kay was greatly astonished then.

He was nine tailor's yards in height, and so it would be very surprising if his legs had not been long and powerful, too. Of the largest of all the posts in that hall, there was none but that his thighs were thicker. His arms were huge, without a doubt, and indeed his fingers, too, which were as big as any one of our legs. Whoever stood up to a blow from his hand was not weak, I know – I can safely swear to it.

Then Sir Gawain knelt down. The Carl said that he might well be a knight, and at once commanded him to stand up:

'Do not kneel, noble knight. You shall lodge with a Carl tonight, I swear by St John. You shall have no courtesy here but Carl's courtesy, God help me, for certainly I have no other.'

He ordered wine to be brought in precious gold, and at once it came in bright cups, shining like the sun.

A cup held four gallons and more; he ordered a larger one to be brought out.

'What is the use of this little cup? This is too small a cup for me when I sit by the fire in comfort all by myself. Bring us a bigger bowl of wine; let us drink, and then amuse ourselves until we go to supper.'

The butler brought a golden cup (nine gallons it held) and gave it at once to the Carl.

Nine gallons it held and more. He was no weakling who carried that in his one hand. The knights quickly drank, and then rose and went out to see how their horses were. They had corn and hay ready, and a little foal stood close to them, eating with their horses. The bishop pushed the foal away:

'You shan't be stabled with my palfrey while I am a bishop in this land.'

The Carl then came up in a great hurry and asked:

'Who has done this deed?'

The bishop said, 'I did.'

'And so you shall have a blow and it shall be well and truly dealt to you, I swear, God save me.'

'I am a clerk in high orders.'

'You don't know anything about courtesy, I swear, as I hope to thrive.'

Then he gave the bishop a blow that felled him to the ground, and there he lay stunned.

In the same way Kay came along to see how his horse was. He found the foal beside him. He drove him out through the door and gave him a clout on the back. The Carl actually saw it, and gave Sir Kay such a blow that it promptly laid him on the ground, and he too lay there stunned.

'Ignorant knights,' said the Carl, 'I shall teach you some of my courtesy before you go away.'

Then they got up and went into the hall, the bishop and Sir Kay, who was a well-built man, too. Sir Gawain asked where they had been. They said:

'We've been to look at our horses, and we very much regret it.'

Then Gawain replied very courteously

'Sir, with your consent, I shall do the same.'

The Carl knew his intention. It was raining and a dreadful storm was blowing, so that Gawain was glad that he had found lodging, by book and bell.

The foal was standing outside the stable door, and Gawain pushed it inside again with his hand. The foal was very wet, I feel sure, for it had been standing in the rain. Then Sir Gawain covered it with his green cloak.

'Stand up, foal, and eat your fodder. We are enjoying what your master earns while we stay here.'

The Carl stood close by him and thanked him very courteously – many times, I believe.

By that time their supper was prepared, and the tables were set up and quickly covered; they would not delay. The bishop forthwith took the seat of honour, with great satisfaction. Sir Kay was placed on the other side, opposite the Carl's wife, who was most richly adorned, and so fair and white. Her arms were slim, her waist slender, her eyes grey, her brows arched. Her courtesy was perfect.

Her complexion was rosy and her cheeks plump – no more lovely woman ever lived, nor was more exquisite in appearance. She was so splendid and so elegant that I cannot describe her clothes. She was so beautifully dressed.

'How sad for you, noble lady,' thought Kay, 'that you should be wasted on such a loathsome man.'

'Sit still,' said the Carl, 'and eat your food. You are thinking more than you dare speak, I can tell you for certain.'

You may all of you be sure that no-one asked Gawain to sit, for he was standing on the floor of the hall. The Carl said:

'Now, fellow: see that my order is well carried out. Take a spear in your hand, take up your position at the buttery door, and hit me right in the face. Do as I command you. And if you drive me against the wall you will not hurt me in the least, while I am a giant in this land.'

Sir Gawain was a happy man at that. He got a spear at the buttery door and took it in his hand. He came in a great rage, and the lord held his head down, until Gawain had given him his blow. He gave the stone wall such a knock that the good spear splintered and the sparks flew from the flint. The Carl said to him at once,

'Noble knight, you have done well.'

And he took him by the hand.

A chair was fetched for Sir Gawain, that noble knight from Britain. He was placed opposite the Carl's wife. He felt so much love for her that he could neither drink nor eat anything of all the supper. The Carl said,

'Gawain, console yourself, for sin is sweet, and that I know and can assure you. She is mine and you wish she was yours. Stop thinking these thoughts and drink your wine, for you can't have her.'

Sir Gawain was ashamed of his thoughts. The Carl's daughter, who was very beautiful and attractive, was brought out. Her hair shone like gold wire. Her outfit was so elaborately decorated that it cost a thousand pounds and more. Her clothes were embroidered with rich jewels, with rich pearls scattered about her, a most delightful sight. She shone throughout the whole hall just like a sunbeam – that jewel gleamed so brightly.

Then the Carl said to the girl with the bright complexion,

'Where is your harp that you should have brought with you? Why have you forgotten it?'

Immediately it was brought into the hall, and a beautiful chair was set before her father as well. The harp was of fine maple-wood with pins of gold, I believe; and without interruption, assuredly, she first of all harped and then after that sang of how love and Arthur's feats of arms went together.

When they had had supper and enjoyed themselves, the bishop was taken to his room and with him the brave Sir Kay. They took Sir Gawain – I tell you no lie – and brought him to the Carl's room which was so bright and splendid.

They told Sir Gawain to get into the bed, which was elegantly covered with beautiful bright cloth-of-gold. When this joyous bed was made, the Carl ordered his own lady, who was so delightful to look at, to get into it. A squire came in a discreet manner and disarmed Gawain at that point. His things were taken off in the proper way. The Carl said,

'Sir Gawain, go and take my wife in both your arms and kiss her while I look on.'

Sir Gawain immediately answered him:

'Sir, your command shall certainly be carried out; even, indeed, if you kill or slay me or throw me down.'

He went at once to the bed with great swiftness. For the softness of the lady's body prompted Gawain to carry out his wish on that occasion. The Carl watched carefully. When Gawain wanted to perform the secret act the Carl at once said,

'Whoa there! I don't allow that game to you.

But Gawain, since you have done what I asked you, I must show you some kindness in some respect, as well as I can. You shall have another one as beautiful, to play with you all night until tomorrow dawns.'

He went at once to his daughter's room and told her to get up and go to the knight and not stop his sport. She dared not go against his orders, so quickly came to Gawain and lay quietly down beside him.

'Now, Gawain,' said the Carl, 'do you consider yourself well rewarded?

'Yes, by God, my lord,' he said, 'as I certainly should!'

'Now,' said the Carl, 'I shall go to my room. I give you both my blessing: enjoy yourselves together all night long.'

Sir Gawain was very happy, I can assure you, with this lovely lady. And indeed, to tell you the truth, I believe that the pretty girl was happy with the noble knight.

'Mary, have mercy on me!' thought the lovely lady. 'Of all the knights that have been here, never has one like this come before.'

Sir Kay got up in the morning and took his horse and was for starting for home, I understand.

'No, Sir Kay,' said the bishop, 'we won't go on our way until we have seen Sir Gawain.'

The Carl got up promptly in the morning and found his orders already obeyed and his dinner properly prepared.

The bells were rung for mass; Sir Gawain got up and went to it, and kissed the sweet and lovely lady.

'Mercy, Mary!' said the lovely lady, 'Where shall I see this knight again who has lain so near my body?'

When the mass had come to an end, Sir Gawain asked leave to go on his way, and thanked the Carl for his entertainment.

'First,' said the Carl, 'you must dine and then go home with my blessing, and all go home together.'

'It is now twenty winters ago,' said the Carl, 'since I made a vow to God, for which I was very sorry, that no man should lodge in my castle without being actually slain, unless he did as I ordered him. If he would not obey my command instantly, he would be killed and laid low, whether he were a lord or a servant. I never found anyone, Gawain, except you. Now may God in heaven reward you. And therefore I am very happy.

'May He reward you, who redeemed you at great cost,' said the Carl, 'for all my misery is turned to happiness, through the help of Mary the Queen.'

He took Gawain to a lonely building where there were ten cartloads of dead men's bones, all bloody, I understand. Many a bloodstained shirt hung there and each of them had a different mark on it. It was a pitiful sight.

'I killed these, Gawain, with my helpers, I and my four whelps in truth, as I have told you. Now I shall give up my wicked customs and certainly, no more men shall ever be killed here, as far as I can help it. Gawain, for love of you, everyone shall be welcome to me who comes along here. And for all these souls I promise that I will have a chantry chapel made here, with ten priests singing till doomsday.'

By that time their dinner was made ready, and the tables were set up, and covered with clean cloths. Sir Gawain and this lovely lady were both served together and there was much merriment between them. And so the Carl was very pleased. He told the bishop and Sir Kay both to be merry, too. He gave the bishop, in return for his blessing, a cross, a mitre, a ring and a cloth of gold, I believe. He gave Sir Kay, the angry knight, a swift blood-red steed, such as he had never seen before.

He gave Sir Gawain, to tell you the truth, his daughter and a white palfrey and a pack-horse loaded with gold. She was so glorious and so elegant that I could not possibly describe her clothes, for there was no-one so radiant on earth.

'Now ride off, Gawain, with my blessing, and greet Arthur your king from me, and ask him, for the love of Him who was born in Bethlehem, to dine with me tomorrow, if he will.'

Gawain said that he would.

Then they rode away singing, with this young girl who was so lovely and attractive on her palfrey. They told King Arthur where they had been and what wonders they had seen, without a doubt, with their own eyes.

'Now, indeed, I thank God with all my might, cousin Gawain, that you escaped alive and without being killed.'

'And I, Sir King,' Sir Kay said in his turn, 'was never so pleased that I escaped without being killed. The Carl begged you that you would dine with him tomorrow, for the love of Him who was born in Bethlehem.'

King Arthur at once promised to do so. At dawn they rode out, and there was a royal meeting there, with many a noble knight. Trumpets met them at the gate, and indeed there were clarions of silver all ready for the occasion, without a doubt. Harp, fiddle and psaltery, lute, gittern and minstrels brought them into the hall.

The Carl kneeled down on his knee and welcomed the king ceremonially with wise, well-chosen words. When the king was conducted into the hall there was nothing wanting there that any man could think of. The walls gleamed like glass, with a diamond pattern worked in the colours of gold, azure and grey; with canopies all round the hall, that had pinnacles strongly made from gold. No man could estimate their worth. Trumpets sounded with great fervour, the king had grace said and went to dine, and was served without delay. Swans, pheasants and cranes, partridges, plovers and curlew were set before the king.

The Carl said to the king:

'Enjoy yourself. You get no other courtesy here, I can assure you.'

At that, bowls of gold were brought in, so huge that there was no knight sitting at the table who could lift them with one hand. The king declared:

'By St Michael, this dinner pleases me as well as any that I have ever had.'

He dubbed him knight in the morning, and at once gave him the country of Carlisle, so that he could be lord of that land.

'Here I make you this very moment a knight of the Round Table, and your name shall be Carlisle.'

In the morning, as soon as it was daylight, Sir Gawain was married to the lovely lady who was so beautiful to look at.

Then the Carl was happy and joyful and thanked the king many times over, I can assure you. He had a rich feast prepared, which lasted for a whole fortnight, with games, amusements and entertainments. The minstrels had generous gifts so that they were the better off for spending for many a day. And when the feast was brought to an end, the lords said goodbye before going on their way homeward.

The Carl established a rich abbey to hold services for God's sake, in honour of Our Lady. He had it built strong and well in the pleasant town of Carlisle; it is a bishop's see. And there gray monks were to hold services until doomsday, as I have been told, because of the men that he had killed, of course.

Jesus Christ, bring us to your bliss in heaven above, in your see.

Amen.

Sir Gawain and the Carl of Carlisle, ed. A. Kurvinen, Helsinki, 1951.
(See also *Middle English Verse Romances*, ed. Donald B. Sands, New York 1986, p. 348.)

The Turke and Gowin

Like *The Green Knight* and *Sir Gawain and the Carl of Carlisle*, this poem, dating from about 1500, is preserved in the Percy Folio. In it, the challenge and beheading topoi are combined with three tests in the land of giants. The turk (a hunchback or dwarf, rather than a native of Turkey) arrives at Arthur's court as a hostile challenger, who later becomes a helpful ally to Gawain in the contest with the giants, before decapitation finally restores him to his former shape as a handsome knight. The editors of *Bishop Percy's Folio Manuscript* suggest that the opening scene is probably borrowed from *Sir Gawain and the Green Knight*, and imperfectly amalgamated with the main story, adding that 'the proposed exchange of buffets is apparently forgotten altogether as the story proceeds. Instead of Sir Gawain's *receiving* in his turn a blow, the Turk implores and persuades him to *give* another – he offers him the other cheek.'

Listen, lords great and small,
what adventures did befall
in England, where hath beene
of knights that held the round table
which were doughty and profittable,
of kempys[1] cruell and keene.

All England both East and west,
lords and ladyes of the best,
they busked and made them bowne,
and when the king sate in seate, –
lords served him att his mete, –
into the hall a burne there cane[2]:

He was not hye, but he was broad,
and like a turke he was made
both legg and thye,
and said, 'is there any will, as a brother,
to give a buffett and take another,
giff any soe hardy bee?'

Then spake sir Kay, that crabbed knight,
and said, 'man, thou seemest not soe wight,
if thou be not adread,

1 warriors. 2 a man . . . came.

for there beene knights within this hall
with a buffett will garr thee fall,
and grope thee to the ground.

'Give thou be never soe stalworth of hand
I shall bring thee to the ground,
that dare I safely sweare.'
then spake sir Gawaine, that worthy knight,
saith, 'cozen Kay, thou speakest not right,
lewd is thy answere;

'What and that man want of his witt,
then litle worshipp were to thee pitt
if thou shold him forefore.³'
then spake the turke with wordes thraw,⁴
saith, 'come the better of your tow
though ye be breme⁵ as bore.'

[half a page missing]

'this buffett thou hast . . .
well quitt that it shall be,
And yett I shall make thee thrice as feard
as ever was man on middlearth,
this court againe ere thou see.'

Then said Gawaine, 'my truth I plight,
I dare goe with thee full right,
and never from thee flye;
I will never flee from noe adventure,
Justing nor noe other turnament,
whilest I may live on lee.'

The turke tooke leave of King with crowne,
Sir Gawaine made him ready bowne,
his armor and his steed.
they rode northwards two dayes and more
by then Sir Gawaine hungred sore,
of meate and drinke he had great need.

The turke wiste Gawaine had need of meate,
and spake to him with wordes great,
hawtinge uppon hee⁶;

---

3 kill. 4 menacing. 5 fierce. 6 drawing himself up.

says 'Gawaine, where is all thy plenty?
yesterday thou wast served with dainty,
and noe part thou wold give me,

'but with buffett thou did me sore;
therefore thou shalt have mickle care,
and adventures shalt thou see.
I wold I had king Arthur heere,
and many of thy fellowes in fere
that behaves to try mastery.'

He led Sir Gawaine to a hill soe plaine;
the earth opened and closed againe,
then Gawaine was adread;
the Merke was comen and the light is gone;
thundering, lightning, snow and raine,
therof enough they had.

Then spake Sir Gawaine and sighed sore,
'such wether saw I never afore
in noe stead where I have beene stood.'

[half a page missing]

'. . . made them noe answere
but only unto mee.'

To the Castle they then yode:
Sir Gawaine light beside his steed,
for horsse the turke had none;
there they found chamber, bower, and hall,
richly rayled about with pale,
seemly to look uppon;

A Bord was spred within that place,
all manner of meates and drinkes there was
for groomes that might it againe[7];
Sir Gawaine wold have fallen to that fare,
the turke bad him leave for care;
then waxt he unfaine;

Gawaine said, 'man, I marvell have
that thou may none of these vittells spare,
and here is soe great plentye;

7 win.

yett have I more mervaile, by my fay,
that I see neither man nor maid,
woman nor child soe free;

'I had lever now att mine own will
of this fayre meate to eate my fill
then all the gold in christenty.'
the turke went forth, and tarryed nought;
Meate and drinke he forth brought,
was seemly for to see;

He said, 'eate, Gawaine, and make thee yare,
infaith or thou gett victalls more
thou shalt both swinke[8] and sweat;
eate, Gawaine, and spare thee nought!'
Sir Gawaine eate as him good thought,
and well he liked his meate;

He dranke ale, and after, wine,
he saith, 'I will be att thy bidding baine[9]
without bost or threat;
but one thing I wold thee pray,
give me my buffett and let me goe my way,
I wold not longer be hereatt.

[At this point half a page is again missing. Then Sir Gawain,
involuntarily abandoning his steed, gets into a boat with the turk, and
they sail over the sea to a castle. It belongs to the King of Man, 'a
heathen soldan' hostile to King Arthur and his court, and particularly to
the clergy. He lives there with his company of hideous giants, with
whom Gawain has to enter into various contests. Helped by the turk,
who is able to make himself invisible, he overcomes them all and is then
asked to do something for the turk in return.]

He tooke a sword of Mettle free,
saies 'if ever I did any thing for thee,
doe for me in this stead;
take here this sword of steele
that in battle will bite weele
therwith strike of my head.'

'that I forfend!' said Sir Gawaine,
'for I wold not have thee slaine

---

8 labour.   9 obedient.

for all the gold soe red.'
'have done, Sir Gawaine, I have no dread,
but in this bason let me bleed
that standeth here in this steed,

'And thou shalt see a new play,
with helpe of Mary that mild mayd
that saved us from all dread.'
he drew forth the brand of steele
that in battell bite wold weele,
and there stroke of his head.

And when the blood in the bason light,
he stood up a stalwortht Knight
that day, I undertake,
and song 'Te deum laudamus,
worshipp be to our lord Jesus
that saved us from all wracke!

'A! Sir Gawaine! blessed thou be!
for all the service I have don thee,
thou hast well quitt it me.'
then he tooke him by the hand,
and many a worthy man they fand
that before they never see.

He said, 'Sir Gawaine, withouten threat
sitt downe boldly at thy meate,
and I will eate with thee;
Ladyes all, be of good cheere,
eche ane shall wend to his owne deer
in all hast that may be;

'first we will to King Arthurs hall,
and soone after your husbands send we shall
in country where they beene;
There they wold . . . abide

[half a page is again missing]

'Thus we have brought seventeen ladys cleere
that there were left in great danger,
and we have brought them out.'

then sent they for theire husbands swithe,
and every one tooke his oune wife,
and lowlye can they lowte,
And thanked the two knights and the King,
and said they wold be at theire bidding
in all england about.

Sir Gromer kneeld upon his knee,
saith 'Sir King, and your wilbe,[10]
crowne Gawaine King of man.'
Sir Gawaine kneeled downe by,
and said 'lord, nay, not I;
give it him, for he it wan,

'for I never purposed to be noe King,
never in all my livinge,
whilest I am a living man.'
he said, 'Sir Gromer, take it thee,
for Gawaine will never King bee
for no craft that I can.'

Thus endeth the tale that I of meane,[11]
of Arthur and his knightes keene
that hardy were and free.
god give them good life far and neere
that such talking loves to heere!
Amen for Charity!

ffins.

From *Bishop Percy's Folio Manuscript. Ballads and Romances*, Vol. I, ed. J.W. Hales and F.J. Furnivall, London 1867, pp. 90–102.

10 if it is your will. **11** make mention of

ARTHURIAN STUDIES